THE PEOPLE BUSINESS

THE PEOPLE
BUSINESS

Psychological reflections on management

Adrian Furnham

palgrave
macmillan

First published 2005 by
PALGRAVE MACMILLAN
Houndmills, Basingstoke, Hampshire RG21 6XS and
175 Fifth Avenue, New York, N.Y. 10010
Companies and representatives throughout the world

PALGRAVE MACMILLAN is the global academic imprint of the Palgrave Macmillan division of St. Martin's Press, LLC and of Palgrave Macmillan Ltd. Macmillan® is a registered trademark in the United States, United Kingdom and other countries. Palgrave is a registered trademark in the European Union and other countries.

ISBN-13: 978–1–4039–9222–2
ISBN-10: 1–4039–9222–3

This book is printed on paper suitable for recycling and made from fully managed and sustained forest sources.

A catalogue record for this book is available from the British Library.

A catalog record for this book is available from the Library of Congress.

10 9 8 7 6 5 4 3 2 1
14 13 12 11 10 09 08 07 06 05

Printed and bound in Great Britain by
Creative Print & Design (Wales), Ebbw Vale

For Assen and Bedic, of course

Contents

Foreword

As a psychologist one gets used to one of three reactions when introduced at a party. Some people immediately retreat fearing some magical insight into their murky and embarrassing unconscious. Others stand their ground somewhat, aggressively challenging the scientific status of psychology. Still others look forward to a bit of free advice on their depression, their child's bed-wetting, and various colleagues' alcoholism ... or whatever.

Three factors account for why people are ignorant about the business of business psychology. The first is the media. Portray a psychologist and you have a neo-Freudian clinician. They are bald and bearded with rimless spectacles and a middle-European accent. They are curious curiosities who make amazing counterintuitive, but stunningly insightful, comments. Their insight is that of Hercules Poirot, the perceptive detective. They are the Sherlock Holmes of the unconscious. They are particularly good at understanding strange motives and pick up subtle clues. Alas in reality they do not exist. Not all psychologists are clinicians and not all have these powers. Indeed "psychological mindedness" as it is called is not even possessed by some psychologists themselves.

The second problem is bookshops. In the UK, we have alas taken over the increasing habit of confusing self-help with psychology. Bookshops appear to have given up trying to sell serious books on psychology. This is particularly true of business or organizational psychology where the world is full of quick-fix, magic-bullet books completely uniformed by psychological knowledge or research. Thus the nonpsychology graduate may form a very strange view of the discipline and what it might have to offer particularly to those trying to manage.

Thirdly, the education system which alas neatly compartmentalizes complex problems into independent boxes dealt with by experts who think differently and are often mutually antagonistic to each other. It is therefore no surprise that business people are confused about what psychology is or indeed whether it may be useful to them.

This book is for the stressed-out, busy business person who wants to be an educated consumer of psychology as offered by authors, consultants, publishers or suppliers. It is expected that this book will be dipped into on planes and trains; in waiting rooms; in airport lounges – even in bed. The aim is to educate in an entertaining way.

But perhaps I should put my beliefs and values on the page. This is what I believe.

1. I believe Freud was right when he said the most important things in life are love and work *(lieben und arbeit)*. They are the source of the greatest satisfaction … and potentially, frustration. Hence the importance of a fulfilling job and a healthy work environment.
2. I believe most people enjoy and benefit from their work. It fulfills powerful psychological functions: it provides a source of identity, time structure, social support, money and status and an outlet for people's hopes, joys, and gifts.
3. I believe in the parable of the talents: that all people have particular gifts and that they should explore and exploit them at work for everyone's benefit.
4. I believe people do not change much over time. For an "adult" in the mid to late twenties "what-you-see-is-what-you-get". People can, and do, change as a result of trauma, therapy, and necessity but it is neither common nor easy. Change is difficult, resisted, and unnatural.
5. I believe in both nature and nurture but am sure that the power in nurture is primarily found in early and mid-childhood.
6. I believe people do (and should) choose jobs in organizations that fit with their temperament and values. I feel people select organizations but then get socialized by them so that, over time, organizations become more homogenous.
7. I believe that there are biologically based sex differences that affect how, when, why, and where people work. I think it is as unwise to deny these differences as to exaggerate them.
8. I believe there are systematic, cultural (not racial) differences between people as a function of where and when they grow up. These are deep-seated, implicit values and assumptions about things like justice at work, the role of bosses, the necessity of cooperation and the need for clarity.
9. I believe that people are social animals and that other people at work are a major source of both pain and pleasure.
10. I believe, as some have rather bluntly put it, "shit happens" in the sense that despite our desire for it, the world of work is not a fully just world where the good (talented, loyal, hard working) are rewarded and the bad (lazy, disloyal, manipulative) are punished.

11. I believe that people should be encouraged to take responsibility for their careers. Managers have a role to play, as does the organization as a whole, in the sense that it provides funds and time, and facilitates. But *you* are captain of your ship and master of your fate and responsible for your own development.

12. I believe that "politics at work" are inevitable. Gossip, power struggles, and intrigue are part of the human condition.

13. I believe that job satisfaction and life satisfaction are highly correlated because happiness is largely dispositional and not exclusively a function of the environment. Happy, contented people tend to be happy with their lot at home and at work.

14. I believe that people need to be taught/trained to be managers. Management is a skill: some pick it up more easily than others but all can learn to be better at it.

15. I believe that while jobs have changed a great deal (and will do so) people have not. In this sense, fundamental truths about how to lead people remain constant.

Management is not about mysterious processes. It involves setting stretching, but attainable, goals and getting all those to whom the goals apply involved in the goal setting. It also involves planning at various levels and putting those plans into action. It involves a lot of communication with many groups (colleagues, clients, subordinates, superiors). And it involves listening and picking up the signals about what is coming down the line in terms of changes in technology, customers expectations, employee attitudes, and so on.

Managers need to assign and delegate work equitably and sensitively. Instructions need to be understood and accepted. Managers have to be, at the same time, supervisor, boss, mentor, and coach. They need to recognize the need to encourage learning and training in themselves and their staff.

They need to know how to hire and fire; how to do a job analysis and write a job specification. They certainly need to understand how to motivate people and know you need "different strokes for different folks". They need to know the power of recognition and praise. And how to motivate people under unfavorable business circumstances. They need to know how to appraise and empower. And they need to know about how to deal with sensitive, stressed, temperamental employees. They need to know the law and how to handle both trivial gripes and serious grievances.

They need to know how, when, and why to discipline. And they need to keep abreast of technology.

They need to be able to do all this as well as have expertise in their area. No wonder it is often stressful, bewildering, and confusing. And why they may want help from a consultant and or an organizational psychologist.

This is a book of short essays: over 60 in all. They might pretentiously be called "thought pieces". They are a sideways glance at managing people. They are inspired by three things: the academic literature of management; stories from consultants, trainers, and managers; and personal experience. They share three factors in common: first, they are psychological in the sense that they aim to describe and understand psychological processes going on in the workplace. Second, they have a tone of skepticism, which may occasionally slip into cynicism especially regarding magic-bullet, simple, fix-it solutions at work. Third, they are hopefully amusing and easy to read.

They have been scribbled on boats, planes, and trains; in airport lounges, anonymous hotels and dreary offices. But they are all about the hardest thing in management: People. Enjoy.

ADRIAN FURNHAM
Bloomsbury, London

Introduction

1. How can psychology be used in business?

The image of the psychologist as noted in the foreword remains in most people's view locked in Dr Freud's Vienna consulting rooms. Psychologists are seen to be prurient "mittle Europeans" trying to explore your repressed unconscious. Psychology is seen as a one-to-one, largely therapeutic business. And psychologists are often thought of as a bit weird.

That may be true, but they are involved in a very wide range of other activities. There are clinical, counseling, educational, forensic, health, organizational, and social psychologists. They have different training for different tasks and there are lots of them.

Some psychologists are concerned with behavior at work. They are variously called applied, business, industrial, managerial, occupational, organizational, and work psychologists. They have been "at it" since World War I. Some people think of them as "time and motion" boffins wearing white coats and hiding in cupboards while spying on the employees. Others think of sort of occupational health counselors who try to help people who are stressed at work. More recently psychologists are associated with people who devise devilish tests of intelligence (cognitive ability) and personality (traits, temperament).

Organizational psychologists have many and varied interests and ask a variety of different questions. Baron (1986, p. 7) gave a typical list:

- Are there actually conditions under which leaders are unnecessary?
- Do female managers differ from male managers in important ways? Or is the existence of such differences basically a myth?
- How do individuals learn about the "right" way to behave in an organization? (That is, how do they become socialized into it?)
- What sources of bias operate in the appraisal of employees' performance?
- Is information carried by the grapevine and other informal channels of communication accurate?
- What are the best techniques for training employees in their jobs?
- What tactics can be used to convert destructive organizational conflict into more constructive encounters?
- How do individuals (or groups) acquire power and influence within an organization?

1

■ What conditions cause people to suffer from "burnout"? What can be done to prevent such reactions?

■ How can resistance to change within an organization be overcome?

■ How do new technologies affect the structure and effectiveness of organizations?

■ What steps can be taken by American businesses to compete more effectively against their Japanese counterparts?

■ What factors lead persons to feel satisfied or dissatisfied with their jobs?

■ Are individuals or committees better at making complex decisions?

But what is their role in business? Most importantly is there evidence that work psychologists can be used to improve the profit margin or the share price? If not, can they do something about morale or general levels of satisfaction? If so, how do they do it? And are they cost effective? Why hire a chartered organizational psychologist? It is all very well having an expensive psychologist as trophy coach for the chief executive and an "Investor-in-People" plaque but are psychologists worth it?

The first thing to point out is that psychological expertise is not restricted to HR and health and safety. In fact, that may only be a small part of what they do. They can be, even are some would say, involved in all spheres of the business. Consider the following:

A. Manufacturing and engineering

The design and operation of manufacturing plants of all sizes, and making many different types of products, can have a serious affect on productivity, morale, and accidents. How do you motivate blue-collar workers doing tedious, dirty, repetitive jobs in grim factories? What effect does noise or background music have on different types of work? Which shifts tend to be more productive, and why? How can we ensure people are more vigilant at boring, monotonous tasks? How can we make employees more accident conscious and make fewer mistakes? What factors should be considered to make dials more legible? What is an ambient work environment? What type of machinery is easy to use?

Ergonomists and organizational psychologists have been interested in these topics since the days of Henry Ford and his pioneering assembly lines. They have, however, been restricted in the public consciousness to funny time-and-motion people out of Chaplin's *Hard Times* or that 1950s' favorite *I'm alright Jack*. Indeed their aim is efficiency ... but nowadays much else besides. They can help to design workplaces and processes to make them better places to work as well as more productive.

Disasters like Chernobyl, the *Herald of Free Enterprise* or Three Mile Island showed how bad ergonomic design could have terrible consequences. Designing manufacturing plants and machines that are staffed by humans is part of the psychology remit. By reducing absenteeism and accidents alone they can be seen to pay their way and effectively influence the bottom line.

B. Research and development

Most organizations are convinced of the need to innovate, to be creative, and to introduce new products. From arms manufacturers to pharmaceutical companies, most organizations know the importance of research and development. They know that those that innovate thrive. People want new products, processes, technologies.

So how to choose, motivate and manage those individuals involved in research and development? Can you train people to be creative or do you have to select them? Are "creatives" in advertising very different from boffins in engineering? How can we ensure that we generate good new ideas; recognize them as such and then implement them? The British are meant to be brilliant at invention but hopeless in exploiting their market value. Could psychology help change this?

Research scientists and creatives are "a bit different"? But how to select the really good ones? How to create an environment that really lets the sparks fly?

Psychologists are often themselves research scientists. They know about the trials and tribulations of that isolated, ponderous activity often marked by rejection and failure. They may have just as much knowledge of what sort of people make artistic creatives, who may be equally important in business as those solid citizens who try to turn brilliant ideas into commercial propositions. Insight is at the heart of the research and development enterprise. It is often at the heart, therefore, of the future of the company.

C. Sales and marketing

There is a psychology of advertising and selling; of market research and marketing; and of consumer behavior.

Again, the popular image of psychology informed marketing is out of date and limited. It usually surrounds that old chestnut of subliminal advertising and its close friend the manipulative salesman. Psychologists have always been interested in propaganda and persuasion and in the brainwashing techniques of cults. The image of psychology is often negative. Psychologists have long been interested in how people remember and forget advertisements and brands, which has a big impact on how to advertise them.

Equally they are fascinated by psychographics or the segmentation of the market on people's interests, values ... and of course what they buy and why. They even believe they can paint a reliable picture of those who choose one brand of car or toothpaste or camera over another.

And they are deeply involved in understanding the seller as much as the buyer – that illusive concept of the sales personality. Salespeople have an amazing attrition rate: in some companies 95% leave within two years. They cannot abide the constant rejection, believing in the end that either their product or, worse, their personality is seriously problematic. So psychologists advise on how to select and train salespeople to make them resilient, hardy ... and hence successful. They have had modest success in this endeavor.

D. Finance and accounts

Can psychologists contribute to the orderly, introverted world of finance? The answer is (of course) yes. Technical, specialist-trained people – often males – often make very poor managers. They have few social skills and little emotional intelligence. Most have never been well managed themselves so they have very little idea of what good management looks like.

Many organizations have a dilemma when it comes to promoting experts into management roles to which they are clearly not suited. All want promotion – few want, enjoy or excel at supervisor or management activities. The role of the psychologists is to help make appropriate decisions as to the best course of action in these circumstances.

E. Information technology

Psychologists have been interested in IT since its inception. Cognitive psychologists are interested in how we store and retrieve information; social psychologists in how that information is used in groups; and applied psychologists in how information is used and abused in decision making.

Psychologists have also been involved in the design of systems to make them more logical and comprehensible to lay people.

IT is a central part of everybody's working life. Consider how, when, and why people communicate by email. What affect does this choice of medium have on relationships? This is a psychological question.

F. Human resources

Psychologists often feel themselves most used in the HR field. They are used frequently in assessment, selection, training, change management, and counseling. Many are used for their *diagnostic* skills in trying to understand the real reasons for particular (acute or chronic) changes in behavior like a sudden increase in absenteeism, accidents, or resignations. Others are involved primarily in the business of *measurement* of an individual's ability, personality, or values or of group morale or team performance. They are frequently consulted on psychometric issues.

Teaching, training, skilling, mentoring, and *coaching* are also psychological activities. There are many interesting and important questions for the psychologist: where, when, what to teach, which method to use; how to balance instruction with practice to be most efficient.

Some psychologists are interested in *psychological processes and dynamics* particularly of the top board. Just as clinicians are interested in family dynamics so psychologists can be useful to help understand, and where necessary change, psychological dynamics of people in work groups.

HR people also use and run systems like *Performance Management Systems.*

G. Other overheads

Psychologists are interested in many issues that profoundly impact the overhead and profit margin. They are interested in corporate culture: how to measure and change it. They are interested in stress at work: causes, consequences, and cures. They are interested in organizational development and knowledge management.

The point being made here is that psychologists are interested in and trained to work with a surprising number of issues in business. If people are the most important asset of any business, and psychologists are the people experts, it is no wonder that their role is – or should be – central.

2. The common-sense argument

Psychology in the workplace: obvious common sense? Expensive claptrap? Faddish bullshit? Discuss.

One of the oldest arguments against the use of any "ologists", but particularly psychologists, in any management capacity is that management issues are common sense. And you do not need some pretentious, expensive, expert to tell you what you already know.

Whilst there are times when the common-sense argument is true, it has various flaws. First, where do you get common sense? If some people appear not to have it, the question is why? It certainly is not codified in idioms and adages that are both vague and antonymous: "Out of sight, out of mind" but "Absence makes the heart grow fonder". "Clothes make the man" but "You can't make a silk purse out of a sow's ear". Of course these contradictions can be reconciled with specifics, but how do you know what they are?

Descartes said common sense was the most widely distributed quality in the world because everybody thought they had a good share of it. (Read: many people are deluded about their insight, wisdom, and so on.)

Second, if things at work are pretty common-sensical – how to be a leader, how to motivate your staff, how to prevent stress – then why do people disagree? Is one right and the other wrong? Could both be wrong? So how common is common sense then?

Third, the very concept of counterintuitive cannot be observed in management if everything is common sense. Hence the enormous popularity of ideas that are counterintuitive. Thus we had cognitive dissonance in the 1960s and 1970s which demonstrated that the more you paid people to do boring tasks, the more (not less) bored people said they were. And latterly, with intrinsic and extrinsic motivation, the very fact of paying people for what they really like to do reduces their satisfaction in doing the task. Not common sense? Then wrong.

Fourth, common sense is a child of its time. It was common sense that women, blacks, handicapped people could not do various jobs. In this sense common-sense could be seen to be a collection of fables, myths, and prejudices or a particular historical period.

The way textbook writers confront the common-sense argument is empirically through a quiz. Of course they are designed to maximize reader error.

Here are some examples from Furnham (2000, pp. 164–9):

But why not test yourself? Are the following statements true or false? Mark them accordingly and see how you rate on the common-sense factor in management.

		True	False
1.	In most cases, leaders should stick to their decisions once they have made them, even if it appears they are wrong.	T	F
2.	When people work together in groups and know their individual contributions cannot be observed, each tends to put in less effort than when they work on the same task alone.	T	F
3.	Even skilled interviewers are sometimes unable to avoid being influenced in their judgement by factors other than an applicant's qualifications.	T	F
4.	Most managers are highly democratic in the way that they supervise their people.	T	F
5.	Most people who work for the government are low risk takers.	T	F
6.	The best way to stop a malicious rumour at work is to present covering evidence against it.	T	F
7.	As morale or satisfaction among employees increases in any organisation, overall performance almost always rises.	T	F
8.	Providing employees with specific goals often interferes with their performance: they resist being told what to do.	T	F
9.	In most organisations the struggle for limited resources is a far more important cause of conflict than other factors such as interpersonal relations.	T	F
10.	In bargaining, the best strategy for maximising long-term gains is seeking to defeat one's opponent.	T	F
11.	In general, groups make more accurate and less extreme decisions than individuals.	T	F

12.	Most individuals do their best work under conditions of high stress.	T	F
13.	Smokers take more days sick leave than do non-smokers.	T	F
14.	If you have to reprimand a worker for a misdeed, it is better to do so immediately after the mistake occurs.	T	F
15.	Highly cohesive groups are also highly productive.	T	F
Answers: 1–5 true; 6–12 false; 13–14 true; 15 false.			

If you scored five or less, why not try early retirement? Scorers of six to 10 should perhaps consider an MBA. A score of 11 or above – yes indeed, you do have that most elusive of all qualities: common sense.

Einstein defined common sense as the collection of prejudices that people have accrued by the age of 18, whereas Victor Hugo maintained that common sense was acquired in spite of, rather than because of, education. It might be a desirable thing to possess in the world of management, but don't kid yourself that is very common. Perhaps a close reading of the rest of this book might help low scorers acquire more "uncommon sense".

Another go! Why not a little quiz to determine potential management ability? Try the simple true–false quiz to determine your aptitude. Many people believe simple management aphorisms. A considerable number of British managers believe that, for nearly all workers, money is the most important motivating factor at work. They also believe, contrary to the evidence, that happy workers are productive workers and that great leaders are born with the "right type" of personality.

Education may not be the panacea for all management evils. It may not be at all helpful to people who lack some basic level of ability. It should, however, discourage people from holding simple, simplistic, naive and even wrong views about how to get the best out of employees. Do you have the ability to manage?

		True	False
1.	Relatively few top executives are highly competitive, aggressive and show "time urgency".	T	F
2.	In general, women managers show higher self-confidence than men and expect greater success in their careers.	T	F
3.	Slow readers remember more of what they learn than fast readers.	T	F
4.	To change people's behaviour towards new technology we must first change their attitudes.	T	F

5.	The more highly motivated you are, the better you will be at solving a complex problem.	T	F
6.	The best way to ensure that high-quality work will persist after training is to reward behaviour every time, rather than intermittently, when it occurs during training.	T	F
7.	An English-speaking person with German ancestors/relations finds it easier to learn German than an English-speaking person with French ancestors.	T	F
8.	People who graduate in the upper third of the A-levels table tend to make more money in their careers than average students.	T	F
9.	After you learn something, you forget more of it in the next few hours than in the next several days.	T	F
10.	People who do poorly in academic work are usually superior in mechanical ability.	T	F
11.	Most high-achieving managers tend to be high risk takers.	T	F
12.	When people are frustrated at work they frequently become aggressive.	T	F
13.	Successful top managers have a greater need for money than for power.	T	F
14.	Women are more intuitive than men.	T	F
15.	Effective leaders are more concerned about people than the task.	T	F
16.	Bureaucracies are inefficient and represent a bad way of running organizations.	T	F
17.	Unpleasant working conditions (crowding, loud noise, high or very low temperature) produce a dramatic reduction in performance on many tasks.	T	F
18.	Talking to workers usually enhances cooperation between them.	T	F
19.	Women are more conforming and open to influence than men.	T	F
20.	Because workers resent being told what to do, giving employees specific goals interferes with their performance.	T	F

Answers: 1 = True; 2–7 = false; 8–9 = true; 10–11 = false; 12 = true; 13–20 = false.

How did you do?

Score 0–5: oh dear! Pretty naive about behavioural science.
Score 6–10: too long at the school of hard knocks, we fear.
Score 11–15: yes, experience has helped.
Score 16–20: clearly a veteran of the management school of life.

Another example is taken from Greenberg and Baron (2003):

Common sense about behaviour in organizations: putting it to the test

Even if you already have a good intuitive sense about behaviour in organizations, some of what you think may be inconsistent with established research findings (many of which are noted in this book). So that you don't have to rely on your own judgements (which may be idiosyncratic), working with others in this exercise will give you a good sense of what our collective common sense has to say about behaviour in organizations. You just may be enlightened. Within groups discuss the following statements, reaching a consensus as to whether each is true or false. Spend approximately 30 minutes on the entire discussion.

1. People who are satisfied with one job tend to be satisfied with other jobs, too.
2. Because "two heads are better than one," groups make better decisions than individuals.
3. The best leaders always act the same, regardless of the situations they face.
4. Specific goals make people nervous; people work better when asked to do their best.
5. People get bored easily, leading them to welcome organizational change.
6. Money is the best motivator.
7. Today's organizations are more rigidly structured than ever before.
8. People generally shy away from challenges on the job.
9. Using multiple channels of communication (for example written and spoken) tends to add confusion.
10. Conflict in organizations is always highly disruptive.

Scoring

Give your group one point for each item you scored as follows:

1 = True, 2 = False, 3 = False, 4 = False, 5 = False, 6 = False,
7 = False, 8 = False, 9 = False, and 10 = False.

There *are* counterintuitive findings at work. Managing people is not just a matter of "applied common sense". People and jobs are complex.

Much depends on the "fit" or interaction between individuals and their work task (and their physical environment, and the management style, and so on). Certainly many people could make a good case for there being almost a total absence of common sense among many managers (and workers) in the workplace.

3. The nature of people

What are average employees like? Coy, capricious, irascible sods (the Hobbesian view) or cooperative, altruistic, self-motivated workers (the Rousseausian view). Is it true that if "you give them an inch, they take a yard" or rather that "treating others with respect and kindness is reciprocated tenfold"?

A modern version of this dilemma is the apparent difference between blue- and white-collar workers. It is widely believed that blue-collar workers are motivated by "threat of punishment" (sacking, redundancy), and white-collar workers by "promise of reward" (shares, salary increase).

Who was it that said if you are not a socialist at 20 (years old) you have no heart, but if you are a socialist at 40 (years old) you have no head? The idea is that as you become older (even possibly wiser) you learn not to be fooled and move from an optimistic Rousseausian view to a pessimistic Hobbesian.

The point is that this view of basic nature actually clouds how you manage. Perhaps the most celebrated work in this field is that of McGregor (1960), who differentiates between two sets of assumptions that managers have about employees. The first is the traditional view of control which he calls Theory X.

Thus, it is argued, the approach to supervision will be determined to some extent by the view the manager has of human nature. If the manager accepts the assumptions of Theory X, s/he will be obliged to exercise high levels of control. If, on the other hand, Theory Y is accepted, less control is necessary (see Box 1).

The theory X manager is at heart a pessimist although he might think of himself as a realist. Most do not start off that way.

Wrightsman (1964) has attempted to systematize the various traditions in philosophic assumptions of human nature. He also attempted to spell out the implicit and explicit assumptions of prominent psychologists and sociologists regarding human nature. Experimental and social

Box 1 Theory X and Theory Y

In essence, Theory X assumes:

- Human beings inherently dislike work and will, if possible, avoid it.
- Most people must be controlled and threatened with punishment if they are to work towards organizational goals.
- The average person actually wants to be directed, thereby avoiding responsibility.
- Security is more desirable than achievement.

Theory Y proceeds from a quite different set of assumptions. These are:

- Work is recognized by people as a natural activity.
- Human beings need not be controlled and threatened. They will exercise self-control and self-direction in the pursuit of organizational goals to which they are committed.
- Commitment is associated with rewards for achievement.
- People learn, under the right conditions, to seek as well as accept responsibility.
- Many people in society have creative potential, not just a few gifted individuals.
- Under most organizational conditions the intellectual potential of people is only partially utilized.

psychologists have attempted to specify empirically the basic dimensions that underpin the writings of philosophers, theologians, politicians, sociologists and others about the fundamental nature of "human beings". In doing so, they have attempted to spell out the determinants, structure and consequences of various "philosophies of human nature". For instance, Wrightsman (1964) has devised an 84-item scale that measures six basic dimensions of human nature in his Philosophy of Human Nature Scale (PHN):

- Trustworthiness versus untrustworthiness
- Strength of will and rationality versus lack of willpower and irrationality
- Altruism versus selfishness
- Independence versus conformity to group pressures
- Variability versus similarity
- Complexity versus simplicity.

Interestingly most business books take a very obvious Theory Y, Rousseausian perspective. They portray management as simple and heroic, and people as logical, altruistic, and fairly easy to understand. Optimism sells: reality alas does not.

4. Work psychology as a science

Psychologists mostly think of themselves as behavioral or social scientists. They share the goals of all science in an attempt to accurately *describe* phenomena (processes, people) to *understand* phenomena, and then to *predict* how things work so that they may exercise *control*.

The scientific method is to attempt to observe patterns, and regularity, and to develop a theory as to how things work. This in turn leads to the development of hypotheses which are tested. Business psychologists, like all psychologists, tend to share various assumptions about research and the acquisition of knowledge.

- Human social behavior at work is orderly and regular: there is a pattern to behavior that can be understood (predicted and measured).
- We can, through observation and experimentation, come to understand the causes of behavior: why and what happens at work and elsewhere.
- Relative knowledge to superior ignorance: scientific knowledge is incomplete, tentative, and changing. It is not absolute and never will be, but it is the best we have at present.
- Natural phenomena have natural causes: no supernatural explanation for behavior need be posited. We do not need or want metaphysical or mystical explanations (astrology, crystals, feng shui) for behavior at work.
- Nothing is self-evident: all claims for scientific truth need to be demonstrated objectively, particularly the claims of business gurus.
- Scientific knowledge is acquired from empirical observation and experiments. No one has special sources of the knowledge. It is often hard work and it can easily lead to refutable if long-held and cherished theories.

So what makes a good (business psychologist) scientist? Various lists have been provided but the following is as good as any.

- *Enthusiasm.* One main criterion is to have fun while doing research. The activity of research should be as absorbing as any game requiring skill and concentration that fills the researcher with enthusiasm. Finding a solution to a work problem is a mixture between a treasure hunt and a detective novel. If the researcher or consultant does not intrinsically enjoy the activity they should try something else.

- *Open-mindedness*. Good research and consultation require the scientist to observe with a keen, attentive, inquisitive, and open mind, because some discoveries are made serendipitously. Open-mindedness also allows people to learn from their mistakes and from the advice and criticisms offered by others. It also means being able to let go of pet theories that are demonstrably wrong. This is most important for all in business. Many feel they have invested too much or would lose face if they changed their mind. The very opposite is true.

- *Common sense*. The principle of the drunkard's search is this: a drunkard lost his house key and began searching for it under a street lamp even though he had dropped the key some distance away. Asked why he didn't look where he had dropped it, he replied, "there is more light here!" Considerable effort is lost when the researcher fails to use common sense and looks in a convenient place, but not in the most likely place, for the answers to his or her research questions. As we have observed, common sense is not common at all.

- *Empathy and taking the role of the other*. Good researchers and consultants must think of themselves as the users of the research, not just as the persons who have generated it. In order to anticipate criticisms, researchers must be able to cast themselves in the role of the critic or indeed the person who has to implement their work strategies. The people (the workers, the management) being studied constitute yet another group inextricably connected with the research, and their unique role is part and parcel of the findings. It is important to be able to empathize with them and to examine the research procedures and results from this subjective viewpoint. Equally it is important to try to remain objective.

- *Inventiveness and imagination*. Aspects of creativity are required in the good researcher. The most crucial is the ability to develop good clear hypotheses and know how to test them. It also requires finding new ways to analyse data, if called for; and coming up with convincing interpretations of results. In short, as they say, thinking outside the box is pretty awful.

- *Confidence in one's own judgments*. Since business psychology is still immersed in the realms of the uncertain and the unknown, the best that any individual researcher can do seems to be to follow his or judgment, however inadequate that may be.

■ *Consistency and attention to detail.* Taking pride in one's work will provide a constructive attitude with which to approach what might seem like the relentless detail-work involved in doing research. There is no substitute for accurate and complete records, properly organized and analyzed data, and facts stated precisely. It does not suit all temperaments inevitably. Research is detailed, painstaking work but often with a big reward.

■ *Ability to communicate.* Scientists must write clearly, unambiguously, and simply, so that their discoveries may be known to others. They may learn to clarify, not simplify. To speak plain English, not jargon.

■ *Honesty.* Scientists and consultants should demand integrity and scholarship, and abhor dishonesty and sloppiness. However, fraud in science and consultancy is not uncommon and it exists in many parts of the business community. Fraud is as devastating to science as it is to all business because it undermines the basic respect for the literature on which the advancement of science depends.

To some, debating whether business psychology is or ever could be a science is a rather charmingly pointless academic activity. However, what is important is that the scientific method is used to investigate psychological questions in the workplace.

5. The benefits of work

Sigmund Freud said that there were two really important things in life: love and work. He and others have pointed out that mental health and happiness can be largely dependent on a happy life at work. *Good* work is enormously beneficial and by the same token *bad* work enormously damaging to the individual.

What are the psychological benefits of a good job or indeed good hobbies and for a good retirement? Work provides money to live by but that is not a psychological variable.

Work provides us with a source of activity: *something to do.* It involves goal-directed physical and mental effort. Too much activity and we feel stressed; too little and we feel bored. Ideally people choose jobs that suit their energy and activity levels, which are determined by ability, age, personality, and health. Work helps to more than "pass the time". It prevents boredom, restlessness, and possible depression.

Work is also a source of *friendship and companionship*. Many people marry those they meet at work. Their friendship networks often revolve around the workplace. Many look forward to "shooting the breeze" with their work companions before, on, and after the job. We are social animals. Solitary confinement is a punishment. Indeed the most frequently cited source of job satisfaction is contact with other people: colleagues, co-workers, and even customers.

Work gives one a sense and source of *status and identity*. For men in particular you are what you do. Your job title, your product, your company all reflect on you. Hence the way people boast about or try to cover up for their employer. Equally it explains the importance of job titles. Jobs and work are a source of self-esteem: people are proud to work for certain organizations and identify with their values.

Work *organizes time*. It gives structure to the day and the week. Holidays can be disorienting as one loses sense of time and work identity. People of all ages like structure, routine, patterns. Even with flextime, early people come in early, late people late. They sit at the same seats in the canteen; they take holidays at the same time of year. All of us are creatures of habit. And good work gives us rhythm, a pattern, a structure.

Perhaps most of all work allows us to *manifest our talents, our creativity, our specialness*. Good jobs stretch one to do good work. It often takes a long time for people to find out what their gifts are. But good work is often a place to explore and develop those gifts. Of course bad work – dull, repetitive, menial – does the opposite.

People like to feel they make a contribution: that they give something back. Work forces the link between the individual and the group. People like to feel valued members of the community. They like to feel useful and part of a greater whole. Good work can do this.

The bottom line is that work is good for both the mental and the physical health of individuals, their family, their colleagues, and the community as a whole. All this is most manifest where people have no work or bad work. Unemployment or being trapped in stressful, dangerous, demeaning jobs can have serious negative consequences.

Getting a good job, one that suits one's abilities, temperament, and values, is therefore supremely important. It is far too important to leave open to chance. Equally it is very important to learn how to manage oneself and people at work.

The enthusiasm for emotional intelligence is partly a function of the realization that self-awareness and awareness of others are crucial and often neglected aspects of work. Emotional intelligence is, at its heart, the idea that people who understand their own and others' emotional states and well-being, and can change them appropriately, have a special skill.

The people business starts from self-awareness. It starts from an understanding first how we ourselves tick. Then how others tick. Then how and why people behave as they do at work.

Work is a pretty important activity for everyone. A potential source of great pain and pleasure. A place to thrive or a place to decay. An activity where we can feel at home, contribute, and explore and exploit our talents.

And good work is well-managed work. A good manager, like a good teacher or a good parent, can make all the difference to a person's life. Good management is both a skill and a gift. It is not easy and never will be. But it is at the heart of all businesses.

References

Baron, R. (1986) *Behavior in Organizations*. Boston: Allyn & Bacon.

Furnham, A. (2000) *The Hopeless, Hapless and Helpless Manager*. London: Whurr.

Greenberg, J., and Baron, R. (2003) *Behavior in Organizations*. New York: Pearson Education.

McGregor, D. (1960) *The Human Side of Enterprise*. New York: McGraw Hill.

Wrightsman, L. (1964) Measurement of philosophies of human nature. *Psychological Reports*, **14**: 734–51.

The aging workforce

Age shall not wither them; nor the years condemn! In 2006, UK legislation will prevent employers letting go "people of mature years" who do not wish to retire. A nightmare or a blessed relief?

People live longer: every generation longer than their parents. They are richer, fitter, and more adventurous than any previous generation. Whilst some love the idea of early retirement on a good pension and endless senior citizen or golden ager holidays and cruises, others relish the idea of staying at work ... till they drop.

Certainly governments who run old age pension schemes want to keep us at work, particularly in old (in both senses of the word) Europe. There are more older workers than ever before: nearly three times as many 40, 50 and 60 year olds than one hundred years ago. And there are quite simply not enough young people at work to pay for their generous pensions.

Around half of all Germans, two-thirds of Americans and three-quarters of Swiss people between 55 and 65 work full time. In 1980 there were about twice as many under thirties as over fifties in the European work force. It is predicted that figure will reverse for the year 2020.

There are many interesting implications for an increasingly aging workforce. Instead of there being a nice correlation between age and seniority, it may well be a mix of ages at different hierarchical levels. Work teams are likely to be much more heterogeneous.

Instead of replacing unskilled blue-collar workers with better qualified younger people, companies will learn to introduce lifelong learning. This means taking training seriously: both soft and hard skills. It means the training budget will have to go up and stay up and not be cut back as soon as the bad times arrive.

But do employers want older workers? Are they slow, doddery, forgetful, and computer phobic? Or are they more reliable, conscientious, and good with customers?

Studies do show that quite naturally, older workers hold pretty positive views about their older peers. Interestingly, the quality and quantity of contact with older workers has very positive effects on younger workers' attitudes toward them. But older supervisors are more negative of older workers than younger supervisors.

So what are the issues? Potential loss of productivity is a concern. But the evidence is that if people are in reasonable health and in the right job for their temperament and values, there is no decline whatsoever in productivity up to the age of 80. What about their *lack of enthusiasm for change and innovation?* The able employee, given good continuing training, is not change averse even at advanced years. As much depends on their personality as their declining abilities. Some 20 year olds are massively change averse; some 80 year olds very game to "have a go at something new".

But what about their declining abilities? It is true that it may be harder to teach an old dog new tricks. Word fluency, memory, reasoning, speed of reactions do decline but for most people only seriously noticeably after 75 years old.

But wait! There seems to be no change in rated productivity until about 80 and yet a sharp decline in measured test abilities in the early to mid 70s. Why? First, there is a difference between ability-test performance and job performance, which may have to do with specific knowledge and well-practiced skills. Older people know how to find and use support to help job performance. But, equally, the evaluation of good performance may change as one gets older.

Four things influence an older worker's ability and productivity. First their *physical and mental health*, which influence all aspects of their social functioning. Next their *education and ability*. The third factor is their *motivation and attitude to work*. Finally, there is the *nature of the work* itself, with its peculiar and particular set of mental and physical demands.

Older workers can bring wise judgment and social competence. Many have greater acceptance and credibility with customers than young people. They have often built up useful and supportive networks both inside and outside the organization. Many enjoy and have got used to lifelong learning and continuing education: "learning a little each day, makes it far easier to stay". And many are marked by old-fashioned values of commitment and loyalty.

Teaching older workers means applying what we know about adult education more carefully. Their education works best when:

- People are taught with meaningful and familiar materials
- People can self-pace their own learning
- People have training on a weekly basis rather than in blocks, that is, *distributed* vs *massed* learning
- People practice with new materials
- People can call on special tutors and peers for help.

Older people tend to have lower educational qualifications having left school earlier. Many of them never had the option of further or higher education and may, therefore, have less confidence in their ability – unlike the me-generation who believe they are extremely talented and deserving. They can be less motivated to take part in work training which they might believe "shows them up". After all, most have fairly limited experience of training. But if the training is adapted to their needs they can make excellent and very grateful students.

The population time bomb in Europe is very simple. We are going to have to pay the price of our relative babylessness soon. And this means various things: more migrants, lower pensions, and a slow ratcheting up of the retirement age. Seventy-year-olds at work will not be unusual.

Anxiety management or skills training

Modern management is about presentations. Thus there remains a thirst for presentation skills courses. These come in various guises from the rather mundane, how and when to use the overhead projector, to the super-star television studio model.

There are still lots of helpful consultants and designers who "help you with your slides". What font to use? Whether yellow on blue is as "author-itative" or "playful" as black on green? Where to place the logo? The ratio of words to graphics?

Power-point obsessionality has replaced overhead projector etiquette and the slide seems all. However the pc-run, multimedia show is taking over. The speaker runs slides and videos seamlessly, changing the mood here and there; the focus or the pace. The skill lies more in the design than the presentation.

Actually, what is more important is to understand how to work the electronics. There are few more pathetic sights than the fumbling and rambling speaker who can't upload, download or switch on their carefully crafted presentation. It is, of course, the real test of a speaker's knowl-edge, ability, and style. Not the impromptu talk but the prepared talk with-out the props.

At the other end of the scale is the deeply people-focused approach. This can be called anything from "presentation" to "handling the media". Presentation is too downmarket a concept, as is "interviewing", so new words have to be found to "sex-up" old products. So we have "Media Appearances" or, better still, "Multi-Media Interfaces" courses. These are often fronted by a slightly "has been" newscaster or anchorman, whose job it is to marginally humiliate you at the start of the day and ingratiat-ingly praise you at the end, to prove the course has worked.

The more senior you are, the more you have to do some form of public speaking: to staff, shareholders, and customers' groups. And we have all sat through enough rambling, tedious, incompetent talks to know that a bad speech can seriously damage your reputation. Equally, most people can recall the exhilaration of a sparkling performance, even though the content was somewhat thin.

But are skills courses what most people need? The most widespread, and for many debilitating, phobia is *public speaking*. Some go through life with little more than a brief, bumbling wedding speech. Others are prepared to do anything instead of speaking in public, even to a group of their friends and supporters.

Some may be particularly impressed by the transformation they noticed in a speaker who turned, apparently, from an anxious, shy burbler into a self-confident, articulate performer who seemed to relish the opportunity to wow an audience and recommended a presentation skills course.

But are the very basic assumptions of a skills course faulty? The assumption is that if people are taught some fundamental points and skills – use of slides, pace of presentation, complexity of story – they will become able presenters. Perhaps this is why so many of these courses seem on the very edge of patronizing.

Another approach is more therapeutic than didactic. The idea is to concentrate on the problem, namely anxiety. For many, public speaking is a sort of everyday, acceptable phobia like agoraphobia. Phobia is fear of fear. It is manifest by acute and chronic avoidance. People "cope" with their fear by avoiding situations that provide it – however debilitating that strategy may be.

There are essentially three types of therapies for phobias: two behavioral, one psychoanalytic. The first is the most dramatic: flooding. Scared of birds? The answer is to march you, trembling and sweating into London's Trafalgar Square, where you are forced to endure a very unpleasant pigeon attack. You learn you can survive it. You learn the fear can be managed ... you are cured! At work this means being forced to give a speech with some help from your therapist for anxiety control: deep breathing, clenching your buttocks, visualization, and so on.

Desensitization aims at the gradual approach. You give a presentation to your spouse, then the family over the dinner table, your favorite and supportive colleague at work. It is a mixture of a practice effect plus helpful, warm support. You learn both *how* to do it and that you *can* do it. But the focus is on feelings, not skills. Manage the anxiety and the skills are easy. This is the favored method of treatment.

The third method is based on the assumption that there, in the murky depths of the unconscious, lie buried memories – nearly always unhappy – about public speaking. The idea of speaking in public is supposed to represent or trigger off certain events, memories, feelings. For men, it might be that your dad was a brilliant public speaker and you had deeply ambiguous feelings toward him. You played the female role in the elementary school play and were later mercilessly teased ... You corpsed, dried, fainted on your first attempt. The therapist's job is to find the associations, repressed memories or unconscious motives and bring them into consciousness to be dealt with. Confront the repression and you are cured.

The moral of the story is this: much of the problem with public speaking among nonprofessionals is not about skill, but fear.

They talk in creativity seminars about "liberation" and "unblocking". They teach a few "de Bono" tricks, but assume – in a charmingly evidence-free way – we are all well above average and just need to liberate our creativity juices.

It is essentially the same point with presentations. The pendulum has swung perhaps in favor of skills training and not enough to anxiety management. That is not to say every stage-struck bore will become a stage-struck star after a shot of flooding or weeks of desensitization, but rather that the place to start is the heart, not the head; feelings, not formatting slides; and dread, not dress codes.

Asking for a raise

It is easy to be outraged when politicians, civil servants, and other public sector employees call for a massive increase in salaries. We have lost trust and faith in so many of our institutions and officials and can be astonished by their gall when they do special pleading. Worse, they often seem like the UK post office directors demanding *more money* at the same time as presiding over *declining standards*.

When senior civil servants in the UK called for a 90% raise there was an inevitable response. A great deal of the problem with public salaries lies, paradoxically, in the fact that they are made public.

Consider the following. You own your own company of 100 people or so and don't let HR dictate to you what should be best policy. You have five options with regard to publishing information about staff salaries.

Make it *completely open:* everybody's exact salary is published annually (truthfully, honestly, accurately). Next, *narrow bands:* people know within say $10,000/£5000 how much each other earns. Third, *wide bands:* same as above except with a wider range perhaps $20,000/£10,000 or more. Fourth, *complete secrecy:* None are published at all and matters are kept under wraps. Fifth, *only some are published and never the grown-ups'*.

We know that problems are reduced when the secrecy option operates. A few people do talk and compare salaries, but it is rare. It is still taboo to talk about such things: sex and death have come out of the closet, but not money in any form.

We know that satisfaction with salary is much more a function of comparative than absolute processes. That is, it is less about how much I am paid than how much I am paid *relative* to others at my place of work, or in comparable sectors.

This means that the contented worker can suddenly become disenchanted and angry about their level of pay when they discover a serious inequity: others paid far more for similar work, or so they think. The problem is that they do not always understand fully the inputs into others' jobs: skills, responsibilities, and time spent. All they see are the flashing pound, dollar, or euro signs. They understand the outputs but not the inputs.

Thus it may seem quite reasonable for very senior mandarins with considerable experience and responsibility to compare themselves with "fat cats" in the private sector who apparently have less education, dedication, and stress. Why should they not receive comparable packages just because they work in the public sector?

Sometimes jobs are pegged against others so as to not let things get out of alignment.

So university lecturers might be paid the same as school principals; or social workers the same as private nurses or top civil servants the same as blue-chip company CEOs. Indeed there are organizations that offer to grade jobs using a points system that looks at all aspects of a job to ensure comparable benefits.

The problem with the whole social comparison process is that it cannot be based on totally accurate information. Thus, looking at these pleading mandarins the manager in the private sector sees their secure pensions, their gongs and honours; their massive administrative support, their generous travel allowances, their risk-free environment and job security ... and concludes these are serious perks that explain their comparative salaries.

Equally, the mandarin peering over the fence sees the share options, the telephone-number bonus payments (quite independent of actual company performance or so it seems), the corporate jet, the benefit package and the supposed freedom of the private sector CEO.

It is difficult to evaluate job dimensions such as risk or stress or responsibility or indeed how they can be measured. Politicians, like pilots, claim their high salaries because they often have a short working life, Governments pay academics poorly because they say they have a relatively stressless life, often pursuing their own interests – that is, are intrinsically motivated.

Atmospherics

How do you design shops and arrange products to maximize sales? Supermarkets know the importance of layout. Shoppers are confronted first by fresh produce to convince them that they need a cart rather than a basket. Then the staples – bread and milk – are often furthest away from the entrance, and each other, to make customers walk the aisles.

There is now a small army of experts who determine what is arranged, where, and why. There are blue lights above the meat counter to make the meat look redder, but yellow lights in the fresh bread and cakes section to emphasize the golden nature of that product. Some products that go together are side by side (tea and coffee, butter and cheese) but dried fruit can be anywhere and Marmite hidden with jams and preserves rather than sharing shelf space with its savory soulmates.

And time spent in any shop is the best predictor of how much money is spent there. So shop designers are in the business of slowing you down and making you walk the length and breadth of the shop to find what you want. Mirrors slow people down, hence their popularity in department stores.

The idea is to increase impulse buying. But researchers have found that you need to get people in the right mood to maximize the effect. The window shopper, the harassed executive and the purposeful, list-driven, pragmatist can all be persuaded to dally, inspect, and purchase when the right mood is created.

So how to quickly (cheaply and efficiently) change mood? The answer is in smells and music. Both have immediate associations. They have been described as emotional provocateurs. They seem to be both powerful and primitive. And they appear to work at an unconscious level.

Studies have shown that if you match music and product, people buy more. Play French accordion music in a wine shop and sales of French wine increase. Play stereotypic German bierkeller music and the Riesling flies off the shelves at twice the speed.

Music has powerful emotional associations and memories. Know an individual and you can induce happiness and sadness, pride and shame, sentimentality and coolness. The Scots fight better to the sound of the pipes; the English to the "British Grenadiers".

Music is used to quicken the heart and the pace (marching music) as well as to relax. Few state occasions or indeed any with rites-de-passage significance take place without music to signify the mood and meaning of the occasion.

But the scientists are now beginning to play with smell or, if you prefer, aroma. It is now perfectly feasible to develop cheap, synthetic but impressively realistic scents of anything you fancy. Baking bread, warm chocolate, sea breezes, new car smell, or mown grass – it is all possible!

These new smells can be pumped into buildings at various points to maintain a consistent pong. And we have come a long way from chemically lemon-scented lavatory cleaner or sandalwood joss sticks.

Smells can make you hungry; or relaxed; or even cross. Some researchers have attempted to use smells to increase sales. They found the best smell to pump into a gas-station minimart was "starched sheet smell". Why? The answer appears to be that garage forecourts are dirty, oily places and that people have a clear concern with the cleanliness of the foodstuff (especially fresh pastries) in the shop. The exceptionally clean association of starched sheets does the business. People's concern disappears and they buy more.

The idea is simple. Smells have associations, some of which are shared. Buildings such as hospitals and rooms like dentists' surgeries have distinct smells that can almost induce phobia. Christmas has its own smell, as does the seaside.

But individuals too have specific smell associations. Thus unique smells like Earl Grey tea, Pear's soap, or particular perfumes can have unusual effects on individuals. And the same smell can have opposite effects on two people. The smell of tea can bring pain and pleasure: memories of boredom and excitement.

We know that smell is generationally linked as a result of shared product experience and lifestyle. Far fewer people bake bread or live in the country than used to. Hence the comforting feeling associated with the scents of warm bread, or cut hay, or fresh horse manure may work on people of only a particular age cohort.

Music and smell work on mood. And moods don't last long, although they can profoundly influence both thinking (decision making) and behavior (shopping). The process can even be semisubliminal: while people are initially aware of particular scents, they remain unaware of how their purchasing behavior is changed.

Scientists are beginning to become more interested in this curious backwater. Those studying attraction (the effects of body odor), decision making, and brain chemistry are curious as to precisely what physiological consequences occur once positive and negative moods are induced and familiar scents are detected. But they still do not know how people are able to distinguish between pepper and peppermint, or how wine tasters do their job. It was not thought of as a very serious area of inquiry until the commercial consequences were spelled out.

It is possible to imagine many positive and negative consequences of increasing our knowledge of the link between atmospherics and mood, and mood and behavior. Some will object to a 21st century version of a new "hidden persuader"; others will be pleased to find someone has thought to ionize and aromatize their working, traveling and shopping environment.

Authenticity at work

Every so often the highly fashion conscious business world needs a new idea or word to focus on. It comes in two forms: economic or psychological. The business gurus like Porter and Peters, and more minor celebrities, come up with a concept that is the economic silver bullet to success: "balanced score cards", "process reengineering", "quality circles" and the like.

But the gurus also know that "people-stuff" is harder and perhaps more important. You have to turn people into true believers to ensure productivity and satisfaction, loyalty and work-commitment. So the psychological concepts are part religious, part philosophical, and part psychological. You need a mission and a vision because you are on a crusade.

An old concept is now being dusted down and repackaged for the business guru: "authenticity". Perhaps the world of business is so full of smoke-and-mirrors, spin and fudge, impression management and advertorials that the concept of authenticity seems appealing.

Authenticity means representing facts reliably and trustworthily. It means being genuine. Antonyms for authenticity are fraudulent and spurious. The word is from the Greek and means to gain accomplishments.

The argument is that people at work should be true to themselves. Authenticity is a state of close and healthy alignment between one's own values and those of the organization. Not what the organization publicly professes, but how it really behaves.

PR, CEO-speak, and HR fiddle-faddle are full of aspirational and inspirational twaddle. Read a mission statement: then see if you can guess the organization from which it comes. People are in business to satisfy their stakeholders who keep them at work. Mission statement hopes, such as being "world class" or "first choice", are a consequence of getting it right, not a cause.

The British Royal Marines' "vision thing" is refreshingly clear: "To defeat Her Majesty's enemy when ordered so to do." No flimflam there. Kill, capture, and confound when the boss says so.

So what are the real values of an organization and can one align one's own to theirs to be happily authentic? Organizations don't have values; senior managers do. And they vary. Hence there is no such thing as organizational culture but cultures. People in HR have a different agenda from those in health and safety; accounts believe in different things from advertising.

Some people feel it wrong or inauthentic to work for a company of whose ultimate product they disapprove. What if you work for an alcohol, fast-food, confectionery or, worse still, a tobacco company? Can good Muslims work for banks that practice usury or should a vegetarian work for a sausage company?

But more than the product or service, it is the values underlying the behaviors that gurus of authenticity say are important. This means working out what the company, or your part of it, really values: does it value equity over equality? Competition over cooperation? Authority over autonomy? And do these values accord with yours?

So here is the game. This can take all day and cost $1000/£500 if you attend a course. What you have to do is clarify your values. And try to be honest. Not too much motherhood and apple pie. If you like power and recognition, influence and affluence, then go for it. Do the same for the organization and see if there is a fit; you are aligned; you are singing from the same hymn sheet. Are you in touch, in tune, or a fish out of water? Does this exercise give you a "wake-up" call?

So you've done your self-awareness bit; the value sort; the matching assessment … and, oh bother, you are a misfit, living a lie. Now you can understand your lack of development, energy or productivity (or whatever). So you have three stark choices: leave, change your values, or change theirs. And we know which is easiest.

The gurus of authenticity (for they do exist) say that when people at work feel the need to restrain their personal style to fit with the organization, their authenticity suffers. Indeed. But doing things you don't want to and when you don't want to is called being grown up.

The basic requirements of a business meeting

It's a popular sport, deriding work meetings. They "take minutes and waste hours"; they are "decision-procrastination-events"; they "diffuse responsibility"; they are "pointlessly self-perpetuating" and so on.

It is the case that the length of a meeting is probably a function (square) of the number of people present and the triviality of the purpose. And it is true that they are often best held having the participants stand up to focus the attention and shorten their duration.

One-to-one meetings ("dyadic interchanges" if you speak psychobabble) are perhaps as common as group meetings and often more important. After all, the annual appraisal, the disciplinary interview, as well as the selection, motivational, and exit interview are one-to-one.

Despite the sheer number of meetings that people do (perhaps have to) attend and chair, very few ever undergo meeting-training. It's a bit like sex: one presumes it comes naturally and that one only has to resort to manuals if something goes wrong.

But there are three crucial features of all meetings, particularly of important one-to-one meetings. No meeting should be without the following: a Specified Outcome, an Agenda and a Summary.

Specified Outcome: The reason why outcomes are not clearly specified is because they are often not known. Meetings should have a purpose. The excuse that there are multiple purposes and outcomes is not good enough. That is true of nearly all business meetings – and activities. The usual outcomes are to inform, to devise, to gauge opinion, and so on. Once these outcomes are specified, it is possible to determine whether, indeed, meetings are necessary in the first place. Outcomes are goals – that can and should be specified in detail.

Agenda: The agenda is the plan; the route-map to the goal. It is the menu. The agenda explains what is being considered and when. It lets you know that there is some forethought. Some chair-people like to deal with the hot/difficult debatable issues first and get them over with. Others tackle them last: exhaust the discussion on easy trivial issues so as to soften up the argumentative when the important issues arise.

All meetings should have an agenda, even dyadic (two people) meetings. Even the appraisal interview should. Agendas can be negotiated and prioritized. They help ensure there is no hidden agenda. They prevent people being hesitant or unsure whether to attend.

Summary: Meetings usually end with AOB in the agenda. If the meeting is short, meetaholics find trivial things to raise. If the meeting is long and tedious and passionate, there are usually no AOBs. But this is an inappropriate way to end. A good meeting ends with a summary. It checks agreement, it helps ensure that people go away with the same understanding, and it helps the memory.

Doctors are now trained to ask patients to summarize what they have heard during the consultation. They know that many are anxious and therefore inattentive or at best selectively attentive. Patients are easily confused into swallowing suppositories, taking the wrong pills at the wrong time. So doctors check patients' understanding before they leave.

Good chair-people should do likewise. The question, of course, is who summarizes what and when? Perhaps each agenda point should be carefully summarized by those individuals who are most involved in "actioning" some decision. Then, at the end, the chair-person or his/her forewarned designate should sum up. The less likely to understand the proceedings any individual or group is (perhaps being foreign language speakers), or the less likely they are to comply with the implicit or explicit actions pre or proscribed, the more imperative that it is *they* who should summarize the meeting or the agenda points.

No wonder meetings are so time-expensive and yield so little. Hold meetings with attendees standing up when there is a genuine issue to discuss. Offer an agenda, keep to it, and specify a desired outcome. And make sure afterwards, by using a summary, that everybody saw it in the same way.

Business presents

Never underestimate the importance of gift-giving in contemporary society. It plays a big part in business. Ask any professional. The economics, the language, the psychology, and the sociology of gift-giving are all the more manifest and important at the peak time of gift-giving, namely Christmas. Indeed, due to the successful commercialization of gift-giving, marketing experts are the new sociologists. Never underestimate the importance of business present-giving in certain countries, particularly Japan. One can be seriously embarrassed if one does not know when, how, and what to give. It could threaten the whole deal!

There are many ways to think about giving. For those with a Pollyanna view of the world, gift-giving is (if you can take the sociobabble) the "feminized ideology of love", motivated by emotions of "nurturant-dependence". Those with a more cynical or skeptical view of the world are quick to quote proverbs with a rather different perspective: "Beware Greeks bearing gifts", "Don't look a gift horse in the mouth", and "He gives twice who gives quickly".

There is something deeply ambivalent and contradictory in the whole business of gift-giving. For instance, gift-givers ostensibly disavow the desirability and necessity of a reciprocal return of present, but clearly expect it.

People often feel indebtedness as recipients of gifts. They can feel pressurized to "return the compliment". Some talk of a guilt trip, or the curious feeling of uncomfortable blackmail. Gift recipients must gauge, above all, the motivation of donors for this is more significant than their taste, perspicacity, insight, and pocket. And then they have to calibrate carefully the response. Calibration of cost, of consideration, of culture.

Gifts fail for three reasons: the motives of the giver are suspect; the object is symbolically wrong because it does not reflect the sentiment or the relationship between the giver and receiver; and because it does not meet the self- or mutually perceived needs of giver and receiver (donor and recipient).

The gift-chooser faces many problems: primarily what to buy; how much to spend; how to wrap it; how to present it. Should the gift be functional or frivolous, should it be shareable (that is, food) or not (clothes)? Hence gift-giving can easily be nerve-wracking because of the experience of getting it wrong. And gift-receiving is also a potential problem: it can demand conspicuous amounts of insincere gratitude.

The wrong gift annoys, disheartens, disappoints, embarrasses, frustrates, and hurts. It can show the donor to be thoughtless, unimaginative and clearly deeply ignorant of the values, tastes, and peculiarities of the recipient.

A gift can create and heighten conflict among members of a family, friendship or workgroup. Gifts can turn insiders to outsiders and vice versa. They can destabilize functioning units by changing the status of people in groups. Gifts can demean, defame, and degrade.

Gifts attempt to confirm identity: they say something about your personality, values, preferences. They can falsely impune and hence cause resistance. They can expose authenticity and inauthenticity.

People try to convert by presents. They give political and religious texts to people of no, or the opposite, belief. Most of all, the presents say more about the giver's beliefs and values than those of the receiver.

Receivers have to decode the meaning of the gift. Is being bought soap or other toiletries a hint about BO? Is a box of fine cigars a message about penis-power, smoking yourself to death, or a sign of your having made it? What to make of a boomerang or body-chocolate? Giving a Mont Blanc pen to a computer nerd or a laptop to a computer illiterate may be a sign of ignorance on the part of the giver or a sign of trying to change them.

What does it mean to be given a tie if you never wear them? Or a red tie if all those you possess are blue? Is getting six pairs of socks a sure sign of reaching your dotage? Joke gifts have the most power to backfire and hurt ... the apron to those who hate the kitchen.

The first major issue with gift-giving is the implication of reciprocity. Hence people feel that they have a forced involvement with others. The exchange becomes a contest or even an ordeal. It is easy to start these exchanges but much more difficult to terminate them. Gifts have to be returned within time deadlines. And they have to fulfil sometime opaque, sometimes transparent expectations.

Gifts can be escalated as bets are escalated at a gambling table. People can be pushed to their limit. There are various solutions to this problem. At work some organizations cap costs. Some families do the same. Interestingly, charities can make a buck or two by defusing escalating gift-givers. They can accept a gift, and acknowledge both giver and receiver.

The second, and related problem, is the balance between sentiment and substance. Essentially, this is the balance between money spent and thought or care put in. A gift to a spouse needs to be high on both – you spend a lot of time and money getting it right. Gifts to spouses must be subtle and significant. They must be mementos or touchstones of the past and beacons for the future. The gift may be an heirloom and an asset. A washer may be high on substance but low in sentiment. Get it wrong and the insult may be lasting.

If in doubt try consumables. A Jeroboam or Nebuchadnezzar of champagne can be happily consumed and forgotten. An unwanted or wrong gift that is permanent may be a constant reminder of a cock-up.

On the other hand the office pool (keep it under $20/£15) is low on both. But the presents must be generic, that is, acceptable to all. They can be funny or novelty items but it is hard to prevent the subtle competitiveness that may occur at these times.

Some gifts may be high on sentiment but low on cost. The artist, the child, the grandparent may make gifts – they give their time and their love. Each creation is unique and is special to the recipient.

And what to give an in-law? These gifts, to be successful, may be expensive but unsentimental. A bike for an adolescent; a power-tool to a DIY enthusiast; a useful kitchen appliance to a sister-in-law. But beware white goods or kitchen functionals. It may be wise to check the exchangeability of gifts to prevent the sense of entrapment that recipients feel. This is particularly the case when giving a present to someone from a very different age group, whose aspirations and values are likely different from one's own.

The ideal gift should delight and surprise. The gift-giver should put in sufficient but not excessive effort. If the effort is clearly arduous, it may put demands on the receiver that are seen as too excessive. The check or book voucher, on the other hand, may be too effortless. The problem is that it puts the onus on the recipient to choose a meaningful gift, which was meant to be the essential task of the giver in the first place. In this sense, money and its equivalents are only half a gift, and thus frequently unacceptable unless the giver cannot be expected to know well the tastes of the recipient (perhaps through infrequent contact).

Research has shown the most acceptable gift for a broad range of giver–receiver relationships. It is the "via media" of gifts, being neither too costly nor inexpensive, demanding some, but not onerous, insight into the general taste and preferences of the receiver. It is widely available in many forms, does not demand too much effort to obtain and is open to exchange. What is this panacea of the gift world, acceptable to young and old, male and female, friends and relatives alike? Why of course, it is the sweater.

The C-word

Senior executives now show their success by having a trophy coach. Some still have a personal consultant who may perform duties somewhere between a PA, a trainer or a strict schoolmarm. The more adventurous, or perhaps disturbed, have a therapist – often called a counselor to avoid embarrassment. And only the poshest, or perhaps the most sinful, have a confessor.

What are the essential differences between a coach, confessor, consultant, and counselor? Cynics might say the price alone: it's a toss up between consultant and coach for the top and both may lead to a mild form of addiction. Confessors are hard to find; but they do offer (weekly) absolution. Counselors come in various shapes and sizes: both senior diplomatic officers and student US summer camp supervisors are called counselors.

The four C-professionals share various things in common. At the highest level they dispense wisdom. Not necessarily advice – there is that odd band of nondirective counseling that positively rejoices in the fact that it does not give advice. They merely help the process of decision making.

At best the C-professionals act as confidants; sounding boards. They provide emotional support and insight. Their aim is to provide a whole range of virtuous qualities: courage, insight, inner-peace, determination, and so on.

And they can all be sought via the Yellow Pages, the web, the local paper and the notice board of the local church. They might have very different training to prepare them for the role.

But the really interesting question is how to choose between them. Some would argue that the different C-professionals are actually so different in outlook and training that it would be hard to confuse them. But a quick look at their CVs or résumés implies very little difference indeed. So the issue remains: what are the "select in" and "select out" criteria? What should or shouldn't they have?

There are three sorts of issue here: the first is psychological, the second experiential, and the third moral. It probably is a good idea that people like, feel comfortable with, trust their "C-person". This is about attraction, chemistry, style, or whatever. The aggressive, time-urgent, fiscally conservative but socially liberal bond dealer probably needs a rather different C-person from the introspective potter or the self-obsessed playwright.

Some are attracted to the certainty of a Catholic confessor, others to the existential doubt of a nondirective therapist. Some like their coaches to be conspicuously successful (à la Veblen), others for them to be a little otherworldly. Some "do" humour, irony – others not. Some want demographic (age, stage, gender) similarity, others a Dr Findlay or Dr Seuss or Prof. Mittel-Europa type.

Certainly all want their C-person to be sensitive, self-aware, and wise. Their job is to encourage self-awareness, to provide insight, and to evaluate opportunities. One might expect that they manifest those attributes in their daily lives. It's a sort of "physician-heal-thyself" problem. The financially troubled consultant, the marriage-troubled counselor, the corrupt confessor just don't quite "cut the mustard".

First, there is the good psychological fit. In the words of Baroness Thatcher, "Can you do business with this person?" Do you like them, feel safe, feel they know what they are doing?

Second, there is the not unimportant issue of their qualification for the role. What is their training, experience, intellectual architecture? In short, what do they know and what is their history of success/failure in their chosen profession? This is more than an issue of degree certificates and course attendance, although this may be a good start.

Most people do not want to be under the knife of a (very) newly qualified surgeon, or be on the plane with a pilot doing his first landing, preferring an old(er) hand, with experience. But a C-professional has experience of – what? The vicissitudes of life, the slings and arrows of outrageous misfortune? The ups and downs of a business career?

Do good business coaches or consultants have to have been in business themselves? Do confessors have to have committed the sin they advise against? Is a retired, successful CEO in a position to be a good C-person? No easy answers.

Most people, however, want the following. They want C-professionals who have experience of doing what they do and a list of successful clients. They want to know that that experience is systematic, salient, and sufficient to enable them to do the job properly. They want to know that it is all more than intuition and that they have some intellectual, methodological or therapeutic processes or framework that guide their behavior. Do the C-professionals have their own C-professional? Have they ever? Why not? A few useful questions to ask.

Third, there is the issue around morality and integrity. Of course one wants a high standard of probity. One expects, quite rightly, confidentiality.

But there is one other important issue – how does the C-professional meas-ure success (or failure)? When is it time to terminate the relationship?

The therapeutic relationship can easily be enslaving. There are, genuinely, many clients who can't or won't be out of touch with their C-professional. They need the reassurance that the C-professional (like the Almighty) is always there – even if only on the end of a phone. Most C-people say they discourage this form of dependence, but it does ensure a full order book. Clearly some "one-man-band", recently retired, C-people are hungry for a long-term relationship with a deep-pocketed client to "tide them over nicely".

Ask the C-person if, when, how, and why they have had failures in the sense that "the project" did not work. Ask them how they know/meas-ure it is or it isn't working. Ask them when the relationship should ter-minate. That should get enough data to make a reasonable judgment about morality.

The C-professionals do differ, sometimes in ways you might not expect. The sensible punter will establish what those differences are, before buying the service.

Canteen capers

Do, to use an old concept, the "association areas" at work make a substantial contribution to satisfaction and/or productivity? Is there any psychological or, better still, productivity consequence to the nature of the canteen, the common room, the coffee area?

Years ago (1957 to be precise), a psychologist called Herzberg made a distinction about work motivation which was well known to managers. He separated what he called "hygiene" and "motivation" factors; the former now more often called "extrinsic" and the latter "intrinsic". Hygiene or extrinsic factors are such things as pay and conditions and the physical aspects of work (office, equipment). Motivation or intrinsic factors are such things as the nature of the work itself and opportunities for growth and development.

The unique thing about this famous "two factor" theory of job satisfaction is that it states that you need more than the extrinsic factors to be in place to get a satisfied and motivated staff. That is, however good the pay, conditions, supervisor, and environment are, they alone do not ensure motivation and satisfaction (let alone productivity). Indeed, all they successfully do is ensure a slide into dissatisfaction or being seriously alienated at work. It takes, so the theory says, the other factor to really do the business. If the work is not intrinsically satisfying it does not matter, frankly, whether the person has a nice office or a sympathetic, caring supervisor, even a good salary.

Despite the fact that the theory has lacked academic credibility since the 1970s, the ideas have bubbled down to management education. Many managers assert, that "comp and ben" are simply hygiene factors: don't pay market rates, don't pay equitably and there is mammoth dissatisfaction; pay in excess of market rates and offer a generous and competitive package, but this does not ensure satisfaction and with it productivity.

The physical environment at work has been shown to be a hygiene or extrinsic factor. Despite what architects, ergonomists and interior designers may assert, having a nice office, good equipment and the like cannot and does not on its own guarantee long-term satisfaction and productivity. One often meets the happy, healthy worker labouring in a dark, dingy environment and the alienated, angry employee ensconced in a state-of-the-art, beautifully designed office.

Churchill seemed to be an environmental determinist. Surveying the bombed House of Commons, he said "We shape our buildings and after-wards they shape us". This is certainly true of the office environment. If you believe the office layout has little to do with patterns of interactions, wait until you move buildings or go "open plan". The best predictor of friendship patterns at work is propinquity. It means, quite simply, those who come into contact most, get to know and like each other.

But one also bumps into people in the washroom, the photocopy room, the stationery storeroom and the entrance. Of course smokers meet like naughty, excluded schoolchildren, outside the building on a fairly regular basis; and quickly form into a social group.

Many offices dedicate rooms for association – a common room, a coffee room, whatever. The question is this: does this room have any notice-able impact on the functioning of the business? Naturally designers say yes. Make the room light, airy, modern, comfortable, with fridge, microwave, and so on and you get happy employees who are more productive.

Various people-ologists (anthropologists, psychologists, sociologists) have been fascinated by social interaction at work: its causes and conse-quences. Certainly people do talk (read, complain) about the physical environment, especially the canteen, and washrooms, as well as things like the air conditioning and lighting.

The "ologists" have made three points about the association areas, specifically the canteen. First, that satisfaction with all aspects – food, layout, varied facilities – is only a hygiene factor. This means that facilities at their very best can only prevent dissatisfaction. On their own they are unlikely to be a source of satisfaction. The idea that great canteens actually increase productivity is alas "pie in the sky". They may, however, discour-age people from leaving the building for nourishment, which may be a plus.

Second, it has been known for 30 years that complaints about the food, the staff, and the facilities in canteens are much more likely to be the result of more deep-seated dissatisfaction than that expressed. In short, it is a symptom not a cause; a litmus paper; a conduit. Just as wonderful facili-ties do not promote productivity, nor do inferior facilities, on their own, promote dissatisfaction.

Third, it is the social contact, much more than the food and drink, that is psychologically important in the workplace. The trouble is that we are creatures of habit. We tend to sit in the same place with the same people, often eating the same food. People can feel very territorial about their place. And they often have strong preferences for when they take their breaks.

Canteens are not only for food. They are places where people schmooze, shoot the breeze, exchange gossip. The more solitary or customer-facing one is at work, the more the need to get support from like-minded peers who know "what it's like". And if one can do this in a modern, clean, comfortable, spacious setting – all the better.

Attitudes to the canteen, then, are a good litmus test of organizational morale. But don't believe that if there are many complaints about the canteen, that is where resources for change should be focused. You get "bangs for your bucks" better in managerial practices than "bangers for your bucks" in the canteen.

Charismatic leadership

Two famous "mittel Europeans", much at the same time, defined the essential features of leadership in terms of charisma. The respective fathers of psychoanalysis and bureaucracy, Sigmund Freud and Max Weber, thought of great leaders as having unusual interpersonal appeal and the ability to rally others by the sheer force of their "magnetic" personality, vision, and eloquence. Through a combination of theatrical charm, believability, and conviction, such leaders inspire their followers to adopt a vision that is more than simple self-interest.

Definitions talk of "extraordinary power", "special magnetic appeal and charm", "inspiring popular loyalty and enthusiasm". It is as if charismatic leaders have a special force they have learned to harness. A third eye, a special scent, an invisible field.

But what precisely is charisma? Can it be taught or acquired? Will it compensate for competence? Is it time bound in the sense that what is charismatic for one generation seems phoney and false for another? Can it be turned "on" and "off" at will by those who have it?

There are lots of synonyms for charisma – presence, magnetism, charm, captivating, hypnotic. It belongs to that annoying category of phenonema where people say "I can't define it but I can recognize it".

A rational view of such charismatic leaders is that they tell people what they want to hear. They are believable, confident, and self-assured. People want to trust their leaders to be honest, visionary, and able. They want them – be it in business or politics – to take their followers into a rich, stable, just future.

And yet we know the world is an unjust, capricious place. Perhaps being pseudo-Freudian, we want our leaders to be *in loco parentis*. We want them to be omniscient and omnipotent (if not omnipresent). Charismatic leaders do the "vision thing" well: they know of a new heaven and a new earth *and* how to get there.

Confidence is sexy. Power is sexy. Sex is sexy. One cohort's view of sexy is different from another's. "Sexy" is probably a consequence of charisma, not a requirement for it.

Charismatic leaders need to "read" their people well to instil confidence in them. They need to know their basic fears and values; their moods and caprices; their hopes and aspirations. And they need to express them succinctly and repetitively in the right words.

Good speakers can not only read the mood of the crowd, they can actually change it. However, the former is a requirement for the latter. They somehow need to physically and verbally embody the zeitgeist of their times and be a symbol of their people.

Churchill was far from sexy, and in 1940 Britain was perhaps in her worst crisis since 1066. But the bulldog-like determination to resist; the steadfastness; the "they shall not pass", the twinkle, and above all the speeches, made him indisputably charismatic.

Martin Luther King was an orator of considerable merit, no doubt learned in the pulpit. He was gifted, good-looking, and highly articulate. And he had a mission just right for his time. Indeed, he had a dream: of a fairer, more just, nonracial society.

Kennedy was youthful, good-looking, courageous. He embodied the spirit of America, the young superpower. And he told his people to give, not to take from their country.

Confidence, vision, insight, articulacy – and passion. Passion is very attractive. The young have "passion". Passion is cognitive energy. It is the stuff of movers and shakers. The passionate do not compromise or back down. They don't bother with the third way or the easy path. They crusade for their vision, their people, their cause. Marvelous stuff: white chargers, banners stretched by the wind, seas opening up. Pure Hollywood.

But there may be a sixth virtue: courage. Courage to challenge the past and the present. Courage to slaughter the shibboleths. Courage to confront the myths. Courage to make requisite changes. Courage to fail. Charismatic leaders nearly always have physical and spiritual courage. Most have experienced and overcome hardship. They know about setbacks and hardship and pain ... but also how to overcome those hurdles.

Six of the best then? They are probably related. Courage and confidence can be related as are vision and passion. But they need not be. And then there is the other question. Born or made? Inherited or learned? Is there an aftershave called Charisma? Probably. Perhaps you can teach people to be (more) articulate. Perhaps you can teach a degree of insight into others. You may try self-esteem therapy to improve confidence. And you can even buy books on ideology to help the vision thing. But you can't buy passion or fake it well.

It's not all-or-nothing. There are degrees *of* charisma but as yet no degrees *in* charisma. Some have it but don't always exploit it. Others don't have it but wish they did. The few have it in sufficient amounts and apply it at the right time. They ride the zeitgeist having partly created it.

Cheerfulness

Both school reports and obituaries frequently use the word "cheerful" to describe individuals. Bringers of good cheer, optimistic, spirit enhancing, good to be with cheerfulness is, rightly, always used positively.

But what determines cheerfulness? Why are some people more cheerful than others? What is the opposite of cheerfulness?

The word cheerfulness rarely occurs in the people professions. Both psychologists and personnel professionals prefer synonyms. Cheerfulness is not, it seems, recognized as a competency – though perhaps it should be. People are not, at least explicitly, hired and fired on their cheerfulness or cheerlessness.

Cheerfulness is a personality trait: meaning that people do or don't manifest it consistently over time and across social situations. Indeed that is what makes cheerful people attractive. They don't fluctuate in their positive attitude. They are not moody, easily disappointed, or positive only about a few things. They see the glass half full and getting fuller.

A few years ago a study was done on groups who had experienced major fortune or misfortune. It looked at the lives of a group of major lottery winners and a group of serious-accident victims who had become quadriplegic. Predictably, the lottery winners showed a powerful surge in their self-reported happiness, positive mood, and optimism, while the quadriplegics became, quite naturally, very anxious and depressed.

But what made the results of the study interesting was that around 18 months after they experienced their major life change, individuals in both groups returned to their previous personal level of cheerfulness. Had they been gloomy before the event, they resorted to that state; and the cheerful returned to their natural level. Thus some lottery winners were less cheerful than some quadriplegics.

Scientists studying the new psychology of happiness – positive psychology – have long known this. Through studies of identical twins, it was discovered that their genetic inheritance accounted for half their levels of happiness. Those who were married; with good friends; who were not very materialistic or avaricious; who had a religion/belief system were also happier than those without. Looks, income, age, and intelligence only made a slight difference.

So cheerfulness is largely inherited. It is not easily acquired and is surprisingly stable over the life span. The slings and arrows of misfortune impede it little. Alas, the opposite is true of cheerlessness. All professionals know of the heart-sinking client; the doom-merchant; the glass-half-empty syndrome. Years of therapy, of state and family support, of time off work, and the like appear to have little impact on their basic levels of cheerlessness.

The Greeks knew about the cheerful and cheerless – they called them sanguine and melancholic. Scholars have noted that cheerfulness has correlates: Joseph Addison in the seventeenth century noted "Health and cheerfulness mutually beget each other".

Cheerful leaders instil their staff with courage, hope, and comfort. They dispel gloom and anxiety. They don't give up. Cheerless leaders are miserable and dejected. They hide away, preferring not to communicate and when they do they infect all around them.

Can you be "too cheerful"? It is said that "if you can keep your head when all about are losing theirs … you have not understood the seriousness of the situation". One does occasionally meet the zealously cheerful – often made so by a religious conversion. Their daft naiveté can be trying. But this is affected cheerfulness – not the real thing – and it is annoying and off-putting.

Cheerful people are stable extraverts; they are dispositionally happy. They are found in all walks of life and bring pleasure to others. But, alas, you can't go on a cheerfulness course, although psychotherapists spend a lot of time trying to make the cheerless see the world rather differently. One could even see cognitive behavior therapy as an attempt to change the dispositionally cheerless.

Cheerfulness is a refreshingly psychobabble-free concept. Everybody knows what it means. Few don't want a cheerful boss, colleague, and subordinate. Perhaps it's something worth selecting for at work. People certainly select for it in a spouse and de-select its opposite. Ask about it in references, put it as a behavioral rating on 360° feedback, make it mandatory for promotion. It's good for everyone so let's make sure we have lots if it.

Choosing a futurologist

As astrologers and tea-leaf readers know well, there is little as enthralling as being able to foretell, or peer into, the future. We all want to live in a stable, predictable, and orderly world. To know "what is coming down the line" is deeply attractive as well as reassuring.

Politicians, priests, and pundits are all in the future business. Their job is to see, indeed perhaps to influence, the future and explain, with equal confidence, why what they predicted did not come to pass.

The hunger and demand for those who can foretell the future has of course produced a supply. Astrologers, numerologists, and a staggering array of futurologists have "earned a good crust" describing what is round the corner. They are consulted by an unlikely range of people, from royals to rogues.

But there is now a new market in futurology: business futurologists. They claim to take the guessing out of planning. They promise you that you do not have to be a victim of the future. Futurologists are now so numerous, they have formed themselves into societies like the World Future Society and the Copenhagen Institute of Future Studies. Apparently, they get together to swap stories and no doubt plagiarize a few good ideas and slides.

But futurology is not an experimental science. The "data" of futurologists are a curious mix of rather dreary and often suspect government-collected statistics on population demographics and "soft" attitude poll stuff. So they notice that the populations of the developed world are less homogeneous; they observe birth-rate decline; and they talk about diversity and what that may mean in the workplace. They also see figures on voting and trust in institutions, and conclude we are bored with democracy. Post-millennial children will ask, "What is the point of our country?" and other such mind-bending questions.

But the doyens of the futurologists are the techno-wizards. They talk about joined-up technology, of the web, of biometrics, and they scare the hell out of most people. For them, 1984 has been and gone. Big Brother really knows all about you: where you are and where you've been; your money; your health; your "little predilections". Known already to the powerful and easily shared, this is frightening indeed.

Business futurologists are curiously like hell-fire preachers. They offer a glimpse of a very undesirable future. As one put it "If you think things are under control, you are not going fast enough". Customers are more empowered and demanding; the government more meddling; the workforce less loyal; the technology terrifying.

The idea is they really "rattle your cage". Nothing is safe, secure, sacred. All is in flux. At this point even the gung-ho, 30-year-old MBA, technocratic manager wonders about downshifting, early retirement, and the like. But the clever futurologists then offer salvation, which not surprisingly may involve going on one of their courses, or at least buying the book.

Interestingly, unlike management consultants and business-book writers, who offer simplistic, naive solutions to immensely complex problems and who flaunt wild optimism, the futurologists are for the most part pessimists. Things generally are getting more difficult and complex. All that change stuff is alarming.

But how to evaluate futurology? How to choose a personal business futurologist? How to resolve disputes, incongruities, and disagreements between futurologists? Is it like deciding between different astrologers or graphologists? Astrological predictions and graphological readings are often so vague and imprecise as to make it possible to reconcile practically anything.

Futurologists can be proved wrong retrospectively. It's great fun looking at pre-millennium forecasts from as late as 1995 for what the momentous year 2000 would bring. Many of the predictions now look laughably wrong and pathetically off course. Some came true, but perhaps no more than would be expected by chance.

Thus, if you say there will be a major terrorist incident, a scientific breakthrough, and a sickness epidemic next year, you are bound to be right. The vaguer the prediction, the better. Naturally, futurologists and their fellow travelers have wonderfully distorted memories of their successes and failures. They solemnly list all those (blindingly obvious) predictions which (sort of) materialized and repress/forget/ignore or overlook those that conspicuously did not.

But whom to follow? One criterion could be success in the past. Another could be the quality and quantity of data used to extrapolate findings. But people choose their futurologists like they choose their newspapers. We like our prejudices and world views endorsed. Technocrats prefer futurologists who predict that technology will liberate us from all chores even if it will mean we are under perpetual surveillance. Depressives prefer futurologists who see global warming, meteor smashing, alien invading doom. "Left wing people" prefer futurologists who see greater equality and democracy, and reduced poverty. Capitalists prefer futurologists who see opportunities to expand into new markets.

Skeptical writers and commentators have warned about the business of futurology. The writer Jane Quinn suggested that the rule on staying alive as a futurologist was to give people a number or a date but never both at once. Another, William Simon, said economists put decimal points in their complicated and exact forecasts only to show they had a sense of humor. But it was the famous Mark Twain who summed it up perfectly with the observation that the art of prophecy is very difficult especially with respect to the future.

So beware futurologists' prognostications. A mixture of entertaining guesswork, mildly disturbing visions, and technological tricks. Perhaps an alternative only to Nostradamus and Sci-Fi?

Client gifts and what they imply

Christmas is not the only season of gift-giving. And nor is the activity restricted to other festivals or rites-de-passage. Indeed some cultures operate with constant gift-giving, as any embarrassed novice business person in Japan soon finds out.

In the world of business and government people are increasingly supersensitive to gifts, be they specific goods, tickets to sports or entertainment functions or simple (but expensive) meals. Indeed in some worlds people are required to accurately log exactly *what* is given to *whom* and *when*. And its approximate *value*. The gift is no longer a simple token of appreciation or friendship. It is an object of suspicion, deeply symbolic and potentially dangerous.

Patients give their doctors and therapists gifts. Schoolchildren ritually thank their schoolteacher with gifts. Authors give away their books as gifts – or is this advertising? People in business may receive very serious gifts from their preferred suppliers. Indeed, many organizations have strict rules about personnel receiving gifts, lest they are seen as, or indeed accepted as, a sort of bribe. The psychology of the bribe, of course, is the psychology of reciprocity. I gift you, you buy from me ... and we develop an ever happier, virtuous circle (if corrupt).

Gifts celebrate significant life events; they express good wishes, they "keep up" relationships. But they fulfil other functions. Psychotherapists – as one might expect – are very interested in, wary of, and often rendered uncomfortable by, the gift. They are interested in the "real function" of gift-giving.

One explanation is the Freudian favourite – transference. Patients may give a gift to try to win favor (or assuage guilt), just as they did with a parent. Or it may be that the gift is deeply symbolic. Thus the gift of an elaborate or state-of-the-art corkscrew symbolizes the client's desire to "open-up" more. A box of penis-sized cigars or a mobile phone doesn't require too much imagination.

Therapists say, with their supersensitive eye on paradox (hypocrisy) that the act of giving (generously) can be a denial of the accusation of hoarding, meanness, or greed. A gift may be a protection against fear of anger or sexuality. The client is angry toward the therapist; denies it and gives a lavish gift to disguise it – or rather because they have themselves not recognized their anger. The same is true (of course) with sex – you give gifts to those you fancy.

Alternatively, the gift may simply express an inadequacy with words: show rather than tell. Or it could be a subtly disguised demand for reciprocity from the therapist – I give, you give. I want to know more about you.

So some therapists politely refuse all gifts because they endanger the process. They talk about gifts blurring boundaries, about getting that "uh-oh" feeling, of a warning flag. Certainly most feel very costly gifts are simply unacceptable. And many are quick to see the manipulative quality of the gift. Also gifts given too often are also a bad sign – perhaps for everyone.

Gifts can be tangible or intangible, big or small, of great or little monetary value. Typical things include handmade items, consumables, flowers, plants, books, artwork.

The questions are *when* is it given, *why* is it given, *whether* to accept it and *if* it should be discussed. Gifts are given in therapy at the beginning, end, or middle of the process; on holidays or to represent special occasions in the therapist's or client's life.

But why do some give and others not? Many reasons of course. On the superficial level they represent, quite simply, appreciation or gratitude. More menacingly, they represent an attempt to manipulate therapists into doing, feeling, or thinking something (different). A gift could be seen (as above) to symbolize therapy work – gaining insight, confidence, courage, forgiveness. Some, perhaps most, clients want to feel special, remembered (even, alas, treasured) and hopefully a valuable, used or displayed gift will do just that.

Gifts equalize power: they put people "in debt". Everyone knows that to woo a woman takes time, money, and gifts. When the appropriate cost has been paid one can expect a return. Those who can't or won't pay feel indebted and thus the more powerful are rendered less powerful. The patient who "gifts" a therapist who refuses to reciprocate has him or her in their debt.

If the recipient feels the gift appropriate, acceptable, and complex-free, it is not a problem to accept it. It may be used, recycled, junked, sorted, or displayed. Each in turn of course reflects the real reaction of the receiver.

But should the gift be discussed? In everyday gift-giving, etiquette dictates expressions of surprise, joy, wonder, mirth, and appreciation. But therapists are a bit different: they may want to discuss the client's thoughts and feelings in choosing this particular gift. Naturally they want to focus on the meaning of the gift as they refer to the client's issues.

Perhaps, though unlikely, they may discuss their own feelings about the gift with the client. But remember their job is to listen, not to disclose. They will be wary about the client wanting them to do just this.

It is possible gifts can help the process. They may provide a way to work on the client's issues; they may enhance positive warm feelings. And they may make termination easier.

The moral of the story is this. If you feel at all uncertain about whether or what to give your therapist – desist. It's all just too complicated.

Conscientiousness

Personality psychologists have identified five distinct personality traits, all independent of one another, that help explain (non-tautologically) work, social, and health behaviors. Some of these traits are used extensively in everyday language – like *extraversion* – and used descriptively accurately although few people understand the biological basis of traits. Some traits, like *neuroticism,* are powerfully associated with a very specific range of behaviors like health and help-seeking.

The personality trait most consistently and powerfully implicated in work-related behavior is *conscientiousness*. The trait of school reports, of seminar feedback, and of competency ratings. The data are clear on this trait: it is good for you or at least your company. People high in conscientiousness work harder and longer; they are less absent but more productive and satisfied; they make fewer mistakes and are happy to take responsibility.

There is disagreement between psychologists on two issues and a worrying lack of research on a third. The first area of disagreement is about the trait-word itself; the second about the possible negative side of conscientiousness manifest in the bundle of factors that make up this trait. The crucial, relatively unexplored, and very, very important issue relates to the etiology or origin of conscientiousness. In short, what explains the wide variety of conscientiousness among people?

Conscientious people are dependable, dutiful, and deliberate. They are achievement-oriented and able to delay gratification, and tend to be aspirational at work. They are reliable and responsible, organized and orderly, self-disciplined but not self-indulgent, efficient and ethical. In short, they are very competent. No wonder that the data are so clear: it is *the* trait that is the strongest predictor of any and all work-related behaviors.

But is there a dark side to conscientiousness? What of the overdiligent and overdutiful? Many people at work assume that with regard to many human qualities (like morality, intelligence, customer focus), bias toward action, and so on, is maximally desirable. More is better. But the data suggest differently. You can easily have too much of a good thing. The very moral are priggish, inflexible. The biased to action don't think or plan enough.

So what of the extremely conscientious employee? Certainly the workaholic shows great conscientiousness which may be maladaptive.

The downside of conscientiousness is manifest when people are too diligent or dutiful. Meticulous precision can easily spill over into anal perfectionism. The diligent can easily be rigid, inflexible and desperately risk averse. They can be extremely unbending and unreasonable when implementing rules and procedures. And they can be critical of others' performance. They can equally be supersensitive to inequality and others not pulling their weight.

Conscientiousness is also expressed as dutifulness. The dutiful are eager to please their boss and reliant on others for support and guidance. They can therefore be highly reluctant to take independent action or go against popular opinion. So conscientious people are polite, detail oriented, hard-working, and do things by the book. They tend to micromanage their staff. They try to do everything equally well but they are hard to please. And they seem uncomfortable with ambiguity.

Their task-orientation should make them a valuable team member who will contribute to the achievement of group goals, but they may tend to overlook morale issues. Some of their staff will appreciate the structure, predictability, and feedback they provide, but some will also want more autonomy and the responsibility to implement their own action plans. Staff will usually appreciate their diligence, timeliness, planfulness, and high standards. They approach strategic planning in a detailed and comprehensive manner, however, their plans will tend to mimic those that have worked in the past, rather than incorporating new and innovative techniques.

They tend to overcomplicate problems and issues by seeking the very best solution when an adequate one will sometimes do. Also, when pressured or hurried, they may tend to rely on tried and trusted solutions, rather than seeking alternative answers that they have not used before.

Finally, when they feel a problem is urgent, they may try to solve it themselves, rather than delegating the problem downward, even when it is appropriate to do so.

Critical periods

For psychologists the words "critical period" have a precise and technical meaning. The critical period is a window of time, often specified quite tightly, in which something must occur if it is to have a long-term impact.

Ducks will "imprint" on any object during a critical period, believing it is their mother. They have been preprogrammed to react in this way. Hence it is possible to persuade grey-legged goslings to follow, obey, and imitate humans as if they were geese.

It seems the British love of Marmite is a critical period issue, judging by the way American adults react to it. Unless you have been exposed to Marmite soldiers in the nursery between the ages of one and 3 years, you can never really get a taste for the stuff. It comes as a source of astonishment to the deprived non-Marmite eating peoples of the world that some volunteer to gulp down "salty tar" with such gusto.

There may also be a critical period for learning social skills and becoming emotionally intelligent. Hormone-fuelled adolescents have to learn to charm, to date, to interact. They need to learn to be sensitive to the emotions of others and have techniques for adapting and changing those emotions. Equally, they need some insight into the causes and consequences of their own emotions.

It can be all "sturm und drang" and some young boys turn their backs on all that bewilderment, humiliation, and pain to play with their Gameboys and computers. And they become expert, emerging at 21 years old to be technologically gifted but emotionally gauche.

They may look like Asperger's Syndrome patients. They are not. They have simply missed the critical period for learning social skills. And they may never be able to catch up.

The question is whether there are critical periods in a working life. In many occupations there is the implicit understanding that if you have not done something (usually promoted to a rank) by a certain age you never will. The "passed-over major"; the aged senior lecturer; the forever "acting deputy".

In some worlds, it seems that critical periods occur when one is young. Thus we find wunderkinds going to the best universities in mid-adolescence, if not younger, to study math or physics. Some brilliant mathematicians do their best work in their twenties. Physics professors may be under thirty when they are at their peak. Historians, on the other hand, sometimes mature like good claret, possibly doing their best work in their seventies.

The peak time or critical period for fluid, native or problem-solving intelligence is late teens, early twenties. However, the peak time for crystallized intelligence or general knowledge, vocabulary, and so on, is not until one's fifties.

One way of describing a high flyer is the extent to which he or she is promoted. It is the speed of rung-jumps up the corporate ladder that marks people out as those to watch.

But is there a critical period for corporate education? Better to do an MBA at 28 or 48? Is there a critical period for a job-move out of an organization? Is 6 or 8 or 12 years in the same job too long? Is there a critical period for moving from your speciality (accounts, marketing) to general management? And is there a critical period for being promoted to the board?

An MBA is about certification, about connections (networking) and knowledge. Dons like people in their early to mid-thirties. That is the critical period. They have done a few jobs, probably reached middle management, got a feel for the whole world of business. Late forties is usually too late.

To stay or go? A lifer versus being promiscuous. Fewer than two years looks like capriciousness or a poor choice in the first place. Twenty years, maybe even ten at the most, seems too long. It smacks of being unimaginative, too desperate for security – frankly, too dull.

The question is how long it takes to learn the business and how long to make your mark. Then move on.

Letting go is hard. After all those years of training, as well as the distinctive identity it gave you, at some point you have to stop being an engineer or an actuary and become a general manager. Often an MBA attempts to do this. Specialities are limiting – they railtrack you. Again, leave it too late and there are doubts about whether you can do it.

And of course there is promotion. Being promoted when especially young may backfire – it may send messages it did not intend to. But early and continual promotion is good: indeed it is essential.

Certainly for the MBA and the move to general management, the critical period is probably 3–4 years either side of 28. Do it all too early and you may burn out or not appreciate the experience fully. Leave it too late and you have a fine future behind you.

Critical means just that. It's the window of opportunity. Yes, there are exceptions. Yes, that window can be prized open by the determined with a burglar's tool kit. But for the majority, it means really thinking about one's career, planning sequences and, of course, *carpe diem.*

Cultivating creativity

For management consultants the stress industry is a nice little earner. Everyone likes to believe that they are acutely, chronically, unfairly, and uniquely stressed at work. Further, they are certain that all stress "comes from the outside": that it is caused by others, usually control-freak, demanding and unreasonable bosses.

Seminars on stress are hard work. There is a lot of what Americans call negative affectivity as well as depression, fatalism, and the like. Indeed it becomes stressful for the stress consultants.

There is another more attractive and fun way to earn your daily dollar. That is running creativity workshops. In that evidence-free environment beloved of trainers, people are told that everyone is creative and that they can be taught quite simply to explore and exploit their talents.

The language of creativity-cultivating workshops is particularly interesting. There seem to be five related models. First there is the *muesli* model. People need to *unblock* their creativity. They are in some curious way constipated and unable to let go and express themselves. In this sense creativity courses may be seen as laxatives.

Next there is the *dominatrix* model. Here we are told to unleash our creativity. Somehow one has been bound up, tied down, physically constrained from that most natural and normal of tasks, namely being creative. So courses are liberators.

Third there is the *arsonist* model. Creative consultants and trainers aim to spark ideas and light fires. They see people as dry tinder just waiting for the right moment. Their job is to find ways of facilitating fire-setting ideas.

Fourth there is the *kindergarten* model. The problem appears to be that we have all forgotten how to be playful. Playfulness is apparently not only a lot of fun but it is also very productive. So our trainer helps us regress to a time when we were happy and quite unabashed to draw pictures, sing songs, and so on.

Fifth there is the *jail-liberator* model. The problem, you see, is that we have all been boxed in a sort of cognitive jail that has stopped us … wait for it … thinking outside the box! And here, our happy consultant throws open the doors of our prison and out pops our creative jack-in-the-box.

Note that all the models assume that somewhere and somehow our natural creativity is suppressed. Quite contrary to all that we know about individual differences and human abilities, the assumption is that creativity is not normally distributed: everybody is (potentially) very creative.

Clearly not everyone is musical, or good with numbers, or a natural sprinter. Certainly people can be taught skills and they can become better at almost everything they do. The question is *how much* and with *what effort*. Studies of genuinely creative individuals show not only considerable talent but also sustained effort. Whilst it is true that "good ideas" emerge often in times of relaxation (called the incubation period), a great deal of work has gone into thinking about the problem at hand. Creatives are talented, driven, hard-working – and perhaps rather odd people.

Most creativity courses are fun, whether they are led by arsonists or nursery school teachers. Most aim at "fun and games" and are more about self-concept and self-esteem than anything else. Many people are neither jailed nor blocked, although given the right circumstances they may all display some levels of creative thinking.

Alas, Edison was right: it's all about 99% perspiration and 1% inspiration. Learning to "thought-shower" – the new PC term for brainstorm – in a nice hotel at the company's expense may be lots of fun but is unlikely to do much more than persuade people – rightly or wrongly – that they are very creative.

The dark side of self-esteem

Anyone who works with young people will tell you that "self-esteem training" certainly works. Young people, it seems, have complete confidence in their own abilities and charm but more particularly in their rights. They can be very difficult to manage. Like moody teenagers, they lurch between arrogant hubris and self-conscious humility. They often behave differently with "members of the public", being low on charm.

To an older generation this self-confidence appears more like haughtiness or arrogance. Young people seem not to have been told that it is the meek who inherit the earth; that humility is preferable to hubris and that one should eschew pretensions and presumptions. They neither know nor care that the first and perhaps the most serious of all the seven deadly sins is pride.

So whence this change? Haven't teenagers always lurched uncomfortably between painful lack of self-confidence and overbearing cockiness? Is it just time, hormone stabilization, or a touch of reality in the workplace which gives them a sense of who they really are? Perhaps, but the self-esteem industry has a lot to answer for.

The self-esteem industry is found doing well in educational and counseling circles as well as self-help bookshops. The idea is that teenagers' alienation, angst, delinquency, truancy, and underachievement are all a simple and complete function of the individual's poor self-esteem. And, equally naively, the argument is that all these socially undesirable behaviors can, quite easily, be alleviated by self-esteem training.

Curiously, whatever their demography, physique, or ability profile, young people are apparently in need of self-esteem training. Young blacks have no heroes and a history of disadvantage and discrimination. Girls live in an unfair world that discriminates against them. The fat, short, disabled – you name it – need self-esteem training (therapy) because (and here's the error) the possession of self-esteem is a cause of happiness, adjustment, and self-actualization.

The logic goes something like this: people who feel good about themselves are better citizens – they don't break the law; they take school seriously and learn; they have better relationships; they don't take drugs, and so on. Furthermore, teaching self-esteem is comparatively easy (and cheap). Bingo! A new Eden.

But is self-esteem the cause or the consequence of success? People who are good at things – schoolwork, sport, music – receive feedback on their abilities. And they soon get into a virtuous circle. Their effort and ability get rewarded by success, which builds self-confidence, which increases effort and motivation, which increase success. And up they go.

Does it help, in effect, to give people erroneous feedback about their abilities, performance, or potential? The person – of whatever age – with fragile self-esteem seems very needy. Just like bipolar adolescents, they seem oversensitive to slights and overneedy for praise. They demand reassurance, but can be dismissive. Some go on arrogance-benders. Others resort to complaining to professional bodies about those who were not supportive and kind enough.

The self-esteem industry is fundamentally flawed by that old undergraduate issue of cause and correlation. The link is correctly made between self-esteem and adaptive and nonadaptive behaviors (virtuous and vicious cycles). But self-esteem is seen as a cause as opposed to a consequence.

Much better to find what people are good at and then train them extensively; help them to win and succeed. In other words, let their self-esteem be derived from their efforts and abilities. This will not be capricious nor will it lead to rebarbitive behavior. But it's more difficult and expensive. It's also tricky if the object of the training appears to have few talents to explore. It does however lead to much better results – and the bright, rather than the dark side of esteem.

Downshifting

There is a wide range of euphemisms for reducing the workforce: down-sizing, right-sizing, restructuring, delayering. In essence they mean for many people: getting the flick, being given your cards or, more accurately, axed and sacked.

What's nasty about "being let go" is that it is frequently not one's choice. Despite the fact that technically it is the job not the job holder who is made redundant, many people feel *they* are redundant. All the more so if they are less skilled, middle-aged or in the public sector. Many know they will never work again; or glean the benefits of work: time structure, social contacts, a sense of usefulness, and a positive identity, let alone a hopefully reasonable income.

But there are those in early middle life who voluntarily give it all up. They quit corporate work for the quiet life. They are not downsized by some uncaring, megalomaniac, shareholder-sensitive boss but, happily downshifting, will walk away from their work.

The downshifters come in a number of stereotypes. First, there are the city superstars who can afford to retire often before they are forty. They are only crypto-downshifting. A couple of million nicely concealed in a tax haven, a house in the country, a good sized town house, and a few more (say five) million shrewdly invested make for a comfortable second half of life. But these downshifters are really unlikely to downshift. The energy, the skills, and the values that led these ultra-successful people to achieve it in the first place mean they will likely start all over again. They may retire – and downshift – four or five times in a lifetime.

Second there are the romantic, bucolic types who may be the neo-downshifters. These are victims of the "good life" myth who believe in seventeenth-century ideas about the countryside. Somehow the city and suburbs are places of unnaturalness and bring with them illness and stress. Modern working life is the embodiment of all that is wrong with the West and leads not to health and happiness but alienation and inauthenticity.

So whatever their financial situation – although it is likely to be comfortable – the neo-downshifters sell their comfortable suburban house and flee to some small village that satisfies their dream. It may be a Cornish fishing village, an old barn in Provence, a croft in the Highlands, or a Spanish or West Indian island. But one certainly wants broadband connections. The idea is to live more simply; perhaps take up a new skill; even – yes they still exist – become self-sufficient.

Allied to the *neo-downshifter* and with something of the income of the *crypto-downshifter* is the *pseudo-downshifter*. This lot merely play at downshifting. It's merely a career move. Perhaps they have been made redundant – with a nice severance package; perhaps, they simply sell when property prices seem to reach their peak. These downshifters are just relocaters. They enjoy modern work and the benefits that it brings. Because of changes in lifestyle due to changes in location (city vs rural, England vs Spain), the crypto-downshifters look as if they have made radical choices to change their lives but they have not.

In essence the personal decision to downshift is an issue of push and pull. Some people are pushed to leave their work. They complain they have no time for family, friends, and hobbies. Some complain about being cash rich/time poor: "what's the point of earning all this money if you do not have any time to spend it". They talk about being constantly tired, stressed by deadlines, demanding bosses, and clients, and that work is no longer satisfying. Most telling of all they claim that work is affecting their health and well-being.

These people may be at any level and any age although they will likely be in the mid-forties to fifties, and middle management. With luck their children are mainly "off their hands" and they calculate that with pension, savings, and profit from the house-move they could afford to downshift (not retire) with more benefits than losses. So they may take up voluntary work, a part-time job, new hobbies.

There are also the downshifters who are pulled by the romance of the downshifter lifestyle – although they are unlikely to use the work downshift, which is too negative. For them the change is about a positive choice, discovery, a new and better life. They are *up*beat about *down*shifting and hence may call the change upshifting.

They change because they argue their work does not really reflect their values. Work is about cut-throat, competitive, win–lose materialism, whereas they believe in caring and sharing, cooperation, win–win humanism (or some such guru-speak). They might even talk about their feelings of inadequacy with respect to their contribution to society.

They believe in a simpler, different life where people are different. Nearly always this is in smaller communities, in the country, where older (read better) ways prevail. Some may be motivated by religious, political or other ideological beliefs that part inspire both the vision and the place sought. But it is not a course requirement.

The pushed and pulled downshifters, be they neo-, pseudo-, or crypto-, are happy to discuss the money–happiness link. Some of them have read the data so puzzling (and disappointing) to economists which show quite clearly that over the past fifty years in the West there has been a steady rise in material wealth but no change whatsoever in self-reported happiness or well-being. Happiness is not a platinum charge-card but a good friendship network, a happy relationship, a satisfying job and a sense of the eternal.

So the downshifter may become a zealot for the cause. A psychologist might at this point spot dissonance. The more they miss their Porsche, first-class travel (with consequent air miles), and secretarial backup, the more strenuously they deny it.

It is rare to find no ambivalence in the downshifter. Change and adaptation are difficult for most – except the pushed downshifter with a good severance package.

Education for life

"Education", said the famous American behaviorist B F Skinner, "is what survives when what has been learned has been forgotten".

There is, it seems, a passion for learning (rather than education) in organizations. Hence all this HR-babble about lifelong learning, the learning organization, learning styles, and so on. Is this anything more than saying learning is important?

For many, education is a formal process. It takes place when you are young. It is compulsory, exam oriented, often dreary. Post-school education takes two forms: career-oriented learning and training, or curiosity-based, finishing-school learning.

Some degrees, diplomas, certificates, and the like, are a course requirement for particular jobs. At university, degrees in topics like accountancy and architecture, medicine and mechanical engineering, are clearly career oriented. Sometimes these courses are strictly postgraduate such as education or librarianship. They offer a historical, philosophical, and critical perspective on the whole enterprise. There is more emphasis on knowledge than skills; on thinking than doing.

Other courses are unashamedly about training: about doing. A manual is different from a textbook; a trainer different from a teacher. Training is more focused; more (in the modern jargon) competency based. It does not take as long as education and tends not to ask big questions. It's more about procedures and process than context and criticism.

Some people elect to do a degree or diploma in disciplines with no obvious career associated with them: philosophy or zoology; sociology or history; archaeology or anthropology. They tend to be more in the arts and social sciences. And there are those rather odd new degrees, often with the hopeful, pretentious, and undeserving suffix of "science". Hence we have "information science" and "sports science". Worse, much worse, is the suffix "studies" – "media studies" or "women's studies". They are a hotchpotch of areas, topics, approaches, and methodologies, "ring fenced" to supposedly give coherence.

It's both easy and commonplace to be cynical about educationists. For some, those who can do; those who can't teach. But those who can't even teach teachers become educational psychologists. Sages as varied as Anna Freud and Mark Twain pointed out that formal education has little to do with creativity or learning. Even Helen Keller said college was not the place to go to for ideas.

Lay people and also some educators have a Dickensian model of education, being essentially that the educator pours knowledge from a vast vat into the head of the student. Brainy eggheads know a lot, as they demonstrate on serious quiz programs.

But most educators argue they are there primarily to teach students how to think (within and without the confines of a particular discipline). They need to know how to access knowledge rather than personally store it. They should be able to assess it; précis it; distil its essence. They need to be able to critique poor thinking, research, writing – and do it better.

Education is as much about attitude as process. You have to know what skills and information to obtain before you need them.

Education is not about ideas and creativity although it plays a major part in them. Creative engineers or writers spend very considerable amounts of time mastering their art or science. Creative ideas often occur in the ruminative period when not directly trying to solve a problem.

Organizations are wise to push the "education for life" line. Note, not "training for life". But they need to invest in it all. Education takes resources and time. A small library and an internet connection next to the canteen won't do. Three-monthly educational sabbaticals (perhaps even year-long sabbaticals) should be seen as a reward and an investment for both parties.

The message is that we can never afford to stop learning. Education is ongoing. It is not only useful, it is necessary. Further, it is often liberating and fun. We are nearly all educatable.

Engaging with staff

Good leaders have a clear and accurate sense of their own and their followers' needs. They know that all those mission statement wish lists about commitment, involvement, and passion can only be achieved if the organizational ambience is right. This ambience or climate must inspire people to give their best. That is the job of the leader.

People at work in the public or private sector, in Pimlico, Pittsburgh or Prague, in production or publicity have powerful, universal needs. Managers who understand this and try to fulfil them inevitably have happier and more productive teams. Maybe that is why the concept of emotional as opposed to academic or intellectual intelligence has been so popular.

Everyone needs a feeling of *personal control*, of self-determination, of the idea that they have a say in what they are doing and where they are going. Managers, however, have to trust their staff enough to give them control. The opposite of control, namely powerlessness – and its bed-fellows helplessness and hopelessness – is a major stressor at work. Medical research shows control is closely related to longevity: that is how important it is!

People at work all yearn for a *sense of community,* of belonging, of being part of a group. We are all social animals who thrive on social contact *and* support. People who feel valued, trusted and respected in their workteams form into happy, cohesive and productive groups.

Everybody at work also needs to believe that they personally *make a difference*, that they have an impact on organizational outcomes. All that empowerment talk of the 1990s was precisely about that. People may be links in a chain but each is fundamental, their contributions unique, valued, important, and appreciated.

And allied to this is the need for a fundamental *sense of personal competence*. Robbing people of their self-esteem, their self-belief, and their sense of self-confidence to do everyday tasks has acute and chronic consequences. People of all ages like to feel that they are competent at their tasks but that they can grow, learn new things, and develop. Antipathy to training and change at work lies at the heart of self-confidence. It is a delicate flower as self-help sections in bookshops testify.

The question though is what causes what? Should you concentrate on raising self-confidence in the hope that it will raise task competence or the other way around? People who are good at what they do inevitably get feedback and feel confident. The answer is probably both simultaneously.

Fifth, everybody likes to *have fun*, have a laugh and daily enjoyment. An organization that banishes or disapproves of playfulness stifles its creativity and innovativeness.

Excitement, enjoyment, exploration, and entrepreneurship are closely related. Real laughter at work may be the best index of its morale and a good marker of things like accidents and absenteeism.

And finally there is a fundamental, existential stuff called a *sense of meaning*. People who believe in a cause may not only be prepared to work hard for that cause but also to die for it. Ideology is about ideas and values. People at work need a sense of their work having real meaning and significance above their personal needs. And of course they need alignment between their values and those of the organization.

People who feel that their work is important yet fun, who feel personally valued and competent, and who feel they have control over their destiny often feel what psychologists call a *sense of flow*. They experience total involvement and concentration – time flies. Pay and conditions seem less relevant. It is the nature of the work and the work environment that provide the primary source of satisfaction.

The challenge of leadership is to create the ambience, climate, or culture that makes people feel vital, authentic, and contributing to others in the workplace. No mean task in a big, angry, historically badly managed organization. But that is the challenge ...

Exiting well

It is the sacking season it seems. But someone has to deliver the bad news personally to the chosen individuals.

How should one handle the "bad news" meeting? We know that most managers do not like doing it. Even hard-bitten and hardhearted HR managers often balk at the prospect.

We know that how people are treated at the end speaks volumes for an organization's attitudes to its employees. When somebody goes, voluntarily or not, employees are *super-alert* to how they are treated and how they react. Treated fairly and people are likely to remain loyal. Get the policy wrong, do a bad job, and there are major repercussions for the whole organization. In this sense how people are let go affects everybody, and often for quite some time.

The crucial concept is *dignity*. People who leave feeling ignored, unappreciated, or victimized have their hurt, angst, and anger doubled. Some turn into whistle-blowers, others into saboteurs of the organization's reputation – and equipment. Stealing, cheating, accidents, and absenteeism can go up dramatically.

Some people resign voluntarily. They too need a good exit. They need to feel that they have been valued and their loss will be felt. They need the opportunity for a long chat with their boss or salient others. They need time to clear their desks, collect their possessions, and say goodbye in their own way.

The organization needs to understand their reasons for leaving and any special requests for themselves – and be flexible. More importantly, the organization needs to let them know there will be contact after they leave. They are after all valuable "old boys" or alumni. They must feel welcome to return for visits and made welcome when they do.

Enforced departures may be more difficult. In order of difficulty, it goes sacking, redundancy, and retirement. But the principles for all are much the same.

A well-administered sacking leads to little or no resentment. Ideally the sacked person should feel at least fairly dealt with and that it is the *best option* for both parties.

To do the final interview managers need preparation time. They need to ensure that everyone is singing from the same hymn sheet. For redundancy, it is that reasons are known and shared as to why it has occurred, and details of the package are settled. For sacking, it is that all appropriate procedures have been gone through. There must be evidence and data, and all concerned must be appropriately informed.

The actual interview takes skill. The question is when and where to do it. End of the week may not be ideal because there may be no colleagues to chat to.

The place needs to be private and the layout nonconfrontational. The meeting needs to be formal and polite and, most importantly the message *clear and unambiguous*. This is not the time for small talk. Leave plenty of time for emotional reactions. No flimflam; no beating around the bush.

It takes time for the information and the consequences of retirement, redundancy, and sacking to sink in. Some people seem stunned and immobile and only react later. Some need emotional counseling, others advice, and some a retraining package.

Some individuals *go quietly* and some cause a great fuss. An individual's makeup and values account partly for how he or she goes but so does the organization's exit policy and the skills of general and human resource managers.

There are simply too many tales of people being so badly handled at the end that they turned nasty. They complain of never even being thanked for their contribution, of their pass being almost wrenched from them, of never being asked how they felt, or of a long and protracted fight to get benefits which were legally theirs.

Faking it

One standard argument against the use of personality tests is that they are fakeable and therefore worthless. The objection, however, is never made of the interview: do people never fake in interviews? And if they do, can (all) interviewers detect the deceit?

The faking argument, as regards personality questionnaires, is incoherent, inconsistent, and insubstantial. There are four questions relevant to the faking issue. The first is the most fundamental: what does it mean to fake? Most people understand that faking is essentially lying or, if you are more polite, "dissimulation". But there are lies of omission and commission.

More importantly there is impression-management faking and self-deception faking. The first means people strive to give a good impression which might not be altogether true. The second is much more interesting and serious. It means that people are in some sense unaware they are faking and must be self-deluded.

Most of us know people who (genuinely) think they have a sense of humor. You know they don't. You might know people who are convinced they are ugly, or too fat, or insightful or a good listener and you know that they are not. It is not that they are deliberately lying, raising their profile, or presenting a mask – they are simply wrong about themselves.

The argument that questionnaires are open to faking presupposes that people have insight into their authentic self. That they understand their abilities and emotions, motives and defence mechanisms, ambitions and sources of stress. Then they present a different self that they believe is more appealing to the selector. This gap is faking. But it is predicated on knowledge and insight that people may not have. In this sense, any self-report, be it an interview or questionnaire, is highly dubious.

The second problem is variability. The faking argument assumes a good–bad answer to specific questions: "I can cope with stress well", "I prefer to work in silence", "I am more creative than most people". Yet we know that when people are deliberately asked to "fake good" their answers show considerable variety in their scores. That is, there is disagreement about what constitutes the "correct" answer. If faking is so subjective and a function of the individual personality, so be it: that is what personality tests are trying to measure. And if these varied scores predict behavior, that is all well and good because that is their job.

Third, it is not acknowledged that some things are more fakeable than others. Most people know about two of the most fundamental personality dimensions: extraversion and neuroticism. When asked to, people can spot questions in questionnaires that are trying to measure these dimensions and respond "correctly" to achieve a high or low score. But there is a whole host of interesting and importantly psychological constructs not widely known but of predictive validity. Thus we have locus of control beliefs, self-monitoring, type A/B behavior, repressor-sensitization, tolerance of ambiguity. People cannot and do not fake. We know because we ask groups to fake "good", fake "bad", fake "mad", and there is no difference between the scores.

There are, however, two further objections to the faking argument that should (but won't) put it to bed for all time. The first is that most job applicants don't try to fake. We know this because their responses have been compared to profiles developed by people who know them well and there is very little difference. Yes, some do: because they are self-deceivers, pathetic impression managers, or habitual liars. And there are ways of detecting them.

But the final objection is the most simple and has plenty of evidence to support it. If tests were simply the result of faking they would have no validity: that is, test scores would bear no relationship to behavior in the workplace. But there are sackfuls of evidence dating from World War I to show that is not true.

Where one can measure an individual's work performance, be it positive (productivity) or negative (absenteeism), and where appropriate tests are used, there is evidence for correlations in the region of 0.3 to 0.5, sometimes higher.

Extraverts do better in sales; neurotics don't make good pilots; neurotic extraverts have higher accident records than stable introverts, and so on.

The jury is back. Yes, some studies show weaker relationships, usually because of the way the work performance is measured. It is usually quite a shock for researchers to find that often organizations have no good records on a (white collar) employee's productivity.

The people who think tests can be faked then point out that a correlation of 0.3 means that 0.7 of the variance is unaccounted for. True. But that is not because of faking. And anyway what evidence is there that interviewers do any better? Indeed, all the evidence is that the unstructured interview is effectively worthless.

I rest my case m'lord. Faking by candidate is not a problem when using questionnaires for selection purposes.

Family business

In many parts of Asia (India, China) there is a long tradition of the family business. All members of the family are expected to work in the business which they know, one day, will become theirs. They are very common. Perhaps 80% of the world's businesses are family firms. Certainly only just under half of the Fortune 500 companies are family owned and controlled.

For small businesses from the newsstand to the restaurant this may be a very sensible and economically wise act. It does however attract criticism from jealous competitors who claim family members either "work" for less than the legal minimum wage or else are exploiting child labor laws.

Family members are supposedly reliable, loyal, and trustworthy. They have serious stakes in the outcome of the organization and may be therefore intrinsically motivated. Their foibles, strengths, and weaknesses are well understood. It takes the risk out of recruitment and selection.

It is, in many ways the royal principle: the dynasty model. For thousands of years in Europe, and still in many parts of the world today, the "hereditarianism" principle prevailed. It seemed the natural order of things. It meant people could safely bequeath their life achievements to those who shared their genes.

It is also believed by some that family members are ideally suited to take over a business because of both nature and nurture. That is, having inherited genes from their parents, they (hopefully) have inherited some of the aptitudes and skills required for the business: academic or emotional intelligence; sociability and stability; fortitude and diligence.

But they will also have been socialized and nurtured from childhood in the business culture. They will appreciate and understand from a very early age the importance of customer responsiveness, stock depreciation, profit, and so on. Through observation, education, and participation, they will not only understand the world of business long before their contemporaries but understand it better.

The problems for the concept of the family business lie in many areas. What if there are no children? What if all the children show no aptitude for the business? What if they show aptitudes to work in a completely different business sector? What if there is a squabble, tussle between family members who both/all want to take over the business? What if the chosen successor openly and explicitly disagrees with how the business is doing and wants to take it in a very different direction?

Many self-made business people find it difficult to let go. They also find it difficult to believe that their legacy may be destroyed, forgotten, or reinterpreted. The paradox is this: the ego and energy that were required to start and maintain a successful business can easily destroy it. The autocratic, overcontrolling, dictatorial, oligarchical, alpha male treats his adult, mature children like junior reports long after he should have retired to cultivating orchids.

The concept of the family is of course quite wide. A family business may involve blood relations from various generations as well as relations through marriage. For sociobiologists, the issue is all about gene politics. Parents may give equal shares to all their children but this may not be proportional to their desire or ability to run the company. Remember the parable of the prodigal son?

There appear to be various morals that can be learned from family companies that succeeded and failed over the years. Owner-bosses should understand how and, more importantly, when to retire. This means not hanging on past their "sell-by" date and interfering. It means finding something else to do if the business obsesses them.

Next, it means looking for talent outside the family as well as within. This may mean distant relations or more naturally those who are not related to one at all.

Third, expect and allow others to do things differently. The world changes. The new generation may be more in touch with these changes because they are younger. Their (comparative) youth and adaptability may be precisely what the organization needs.

Finally, when handing over to the children do so equitably but wisely. This means giving shares and control to those who want it and are good at running businesses. Find something else to leave those who for various reasons don't want to become part of the business.

Freudian vocational guidance

The concept of vocational guidance seems so old-fashioned these days. Was it ever taken very seriously, even in the past? Many can remember a rather ineffectual schoolteacher who took pupils through some opaque test or simple-minded interview, narrowing their choices/preferences to something speedily suited to their abilities, temperament, and interests.

Usually, vocational guidance was a decade or so behind the market. Many job types have disappeared; many more types created, but the guidance guys have not kept up. What are the ideal attributes of a web-master, or a senator? The guidance industry in the past made some strong assumptions: the idea of a job/career for life, instead of a portfolio career; the assumption that jobs don't change much; and the notion that all jobs are status neutral, irrespective of their other rewards.

Vocational guidance is always presented as a rational choice. The professionals (dispassionately) assess the individual, conduct the job analysis comprehensively and then (magically) engineer the fit. This seems perfectly reasonable. Yes, people are multidimensional and complex, so are jobs … and things do change … but that is the best way to do it.

Aah … but what about the un- and subconscious? Freudians and their fellow travellers (post, neo, crypto) have always been interested in the "less" rational. While they may not object to the above procedure they would probably do a very different analysis of personality to that of, say, using psychometric tests and a competency-based interview.

Freudians are interested in deep-seated motives, symbolic behaviors, and the role of the unconscious. They revel in trying to explain how people choose particular jobs like being a dentist or a mortician; a podiatrist or a hairdresser; a butcher or a brain surgeon. Freudian theory always surprises. It rejoices in the counterintuitive, suggesting that some behaviors are motivated by precisely the opposite feeling. Thus, the altruistic actually dislike those they help; the ostensibly homophobic is actually gay, and so on.

Sociologists like to point out that job choice is highly constrained. Social class, education, and the local economy put limits on choice. They see social factors and forces limiting a person's options. Thus, as many will attest, years ago girls seemed to have three major career options (only) – teaching, nursing or motherhood. Even today, the sociologists trace origins and destinations to attempt to see career trajectories and how social class shapes and constrains options.

But psychologists, while they may accept the notion of constraints, still ponder on the reasons for occupational choice. Why, they wonder, would one want to become a Trappist nun or a traffic warden or an IRS agent.

Freudians, of course, have an answer. And, as one may expect, the origins are in childhood. They believe adult personality functioning is in part dependent on early childhood experiences, particularly how one resolves or reacts to two fundamental conflicts and dilemmas; weaning and potty training. Yes, to some extent, occupational choice is a function of how your mother treated you.

Thus, to the Freudian, jobs such as tea taster, lawyer, dentist or politician have the same origin. On the other hand, accountants, health and tax inspectors, noncommissioned officers and time-and-motion experts probably all share the same psychological profile.

The "psychosexual theory" of vocational choice goes like this. In childhood we all have to resolve specific crises and the way we do this scars or shapes our personality, in turn making us particularly attracted to (and no doubt repelled by) certain jobs.

The first issue is weaning and with it the possibility of remaining fixated at the oral stage. If a baby is demand fed, given the breast at the slightest whimper, such pleasure means that weaning can be traumatic. Sucking becomes for that individual highly important. From such arise connoisseurs of cigars and wine, gourmets, specialists in oral sexual techniques. They are oral optimists. However, Spock-like scheduled feeding can frustrate this pleasure for many babies. They become oral pessimists. Those individuals later regard eating and pleasures of the palate as, if not sinful, trivial. Those who eat to live oppose drinking, oppose smoking: tight-lipped individuals for whom kissing is a greeting only. Depending on whether frustration was at the early or late oral phase (sucking or biting), food preferences can be affected. Those frustrated at the early stage like soft, milky, sweet, nursery foods, jello, ice-cream, rice puddings. Those at the late stage prefer, bitter, sour foods, hot pickles, raw steaks, curries, Mexican dishes and vinegars.

Nor is this all. In our culture, oral erotism cannot be expressed in its entirety. Blatant expression is regarded as greed, gluttony, and gross sensuality. Aspects are repressed and emerge changed into character traits. Repressed oral erotism (sucking stage) leads to feelings of sociability, optimism, that the world is good, no effort is necessary. Such individuals feel that they are quite literally born with a silver spoon in their mouths. Those frustrated at the breast become bitter, pessimistic, feel that efforts are all in vain. These have a salty, biting wit and again the oral imagery is notable. These oral sadists might be expected to enter the ranks of the dental professions: extractions a speciality.

So oral optimists become singers, radio announcers, tea and coffee tasters, flautists in the orchestra. The mouth is the source of pleasure. And oral pessimists go into dentistry, the law, politics where the mouth is used to hurt, attack, and defend. Orality is related to many choices: smoking, nail biting, choice of musical instrument, vegetarianism.

The next phase is the anal phase: the dreaded potty training. The child's interest in feces turns first to such things as mud, sand, stones, then to all man-made objects that can be collected, and then to money. Essentially, the Freudian thesis may be spelled out thus: children all experience pleasure in the elimination of feces. At an early stage (around two years), parents toilet-train their children – some showing enthusiasm and praise (positive reinforcement) for defecation, others threatening and punishing a child when it refuses (negative reinforcement). Potty or toilet training occurs at the same stage that the child is striving to achieve autonomy and a sense of worth. Often, toilet training becomes a source of conflict between parents and children over whether the child is in control of his sphincter or whether the parental rewards and coercion compel submission to their will. Furthermore, the child is fascinated by and fantasizes over his feces which are, after all, a creation of his own body. The child's confusion is made all the worse by the ambiguous reactions of parents who, on the one hand, treat the feces as gifts and highly valued, and then behave as if they are dirty, untouchable, and in need of immediate disposal.

If children are traumatized by the experience of toilet training, they tend to retain ways of coping and behaving during this phase. The way in which a miser hoards money is seen as symbolic of the child's refusal to eliminate feces in the face of parental demands. The spendthrift, on the other hand, recalls the approval and affection that resulted from submission to parental authority to defecate. Thus some people equate elimination/spending with receiving affection and hence felt more inclined to spend when feeling insecure, unloved, or in need of affection. Attitudes to money are then bimodal – either they are extremely positive or extremely negative.

Money is often called "filthy lucre", and the wealthy are often called "stinking rich". Gambling for money is also associated with dirt and toilet training: a poker player puts money in a "pot"; dice players shoot "craps"; card players play "dirty-Girty"; a gambler who loses everything is "cleaned out".

Families, groups and societies that demand early and rigid toilet training tend to produce "anal characteristics" in people, which include orderliness, punctuality, compulsive cleanliness, and obstinacy. Hence one can be miserly about knowledge, time, and emotions as much as money. These effects may be increased or reduced depending on whether the child grows up in a socialist or capitalist country, in times of comparative expansion or depression, or whether one is part of a middle- or working-class family. Parents' belief in the Puritan or Protestant ethic may also alter money beliefs and habits.

Freud identified three main traits associated with people who had fixated at the anal stage: orderliness, parsimony, and obstinacy with associated qualities of cleanliness, conscientiousness, trustworthiness, defiance, and revengefulness.

So anal people are involved in professions associated with money (accountants, tax inspectors, actuaries) and cleanliness (health inspectors), orderliness (libraries), parsimony (recycling) and political causes.

For the Freudian, the choice of, and satisfaction in, a chosen vocation is at least in part determined by events most of us have forgotten, but which have all left their mark.

Gained in translation

The impressive skills of the simultaneous translator are ever in demand; partly as a function of the remorseless growth of the EC and world trade in general. So we need people to translate Czech into Dutch, Finnish into Portuguese, and Polish into Greek. How long will we have to wait before there are demands for Catalan into Welsh, or Irish into the musical language of the Laps (Sami)?

Written translation is one thing. Simultaneous spoken translation quite another. It won't be long before we will have good computer-generated translations from one text to another. Until then, scholarly language students scrupulously translate dreary policy documents searching for synonyms for "subsidarity" or "set aside".

Written translators are often scholars, but spoken translators need to be actors as well. They have various tasks. Sometimes they shadow their (literally) Great Leader. So, in the old days when we had more than one superpower it was not uncommon to see the American and Russian translators just behind their bosses, subtly, *sotto voce*, and almost ventriloquently informing their man what the other said. Interestingly, the leaders did not look at their co-linguist informant. They smiled, nodded and nonverbally looked at their opposite number directly – and for good reason.

There are also conference (press announcement, business/educational seminar) translators. Many sit in glass-faced boxes like portable confessionals, so that they can see the speaker and his/her slides but not necessarily (certainly not the faces of) the audience. And in this soundproofed cabin, they endeavor to faithfully repeat what is said.

The other type appear "on stage" with the speaker, who stops at the end of every sentence or major clause to hear the words translated. The former is monologue, often monotone, the latter staccato. No doubt audiences and individuals have strong preferences for either type, according to their linguistic ability and the topic of the address.

Few speakers enjoy the experience of translation, as much for what is gained as what is lost. Everyone is aware of how written notices in different languages can take up quite different amounts of words/space. Some languages seem better for certain functions. Hence the British king, George III, purportedly spoke to his horse in German, his cook in French, and his lover in Italian.

The simultaneous translator has to find the right phrase, simile or metaphor immediately. It might not even exist but you can't hang about so a substitute has to be found. And as for jokes … many know they are often unwise and backfire, but can't resist it to liven up the speech.

Good speakers often do puns, asides, and glory in the possibilities of the language. Alliteration can be a very powerful mnemonic device as can onomatopoeia. Some words simply taste and sound better than others. Somehow "lugubrious" sounds faintly ridiculous and "vicissitude" pretentious.

But more than *what* is said, it is *how* it is said. Timing, timbre, and pitch are all important. Watch a dubbed favorite movie with a known star. The dubbing actor may do timings well but quality of voice is crucial. The chuckle, the sardonic laugh, characteristic patterns get changed – and it makes a difference.

Paralinguistic features of communication are so important that some people believe it is as easy to detect a liar on the phone as face to face. Latency of response (speed in answering), pitch raises at the end, linguistic distancing (not using "I", "me"), holding silences, umm-ing and erring all create a powerful impression.

In this sense simultaneous translation does not exist. Translation has a precise meaning and a precise process. Psychologists do back translations to ensure nothing is lost or gained. The questionnaire is translated from language A to B by a fluent cross-cultural traveler. A different person from a similar background translates from B to A. The scientist compares the two versions of A.

Translators, at best, get the gist of what is being said. But they can't do how it is said. Can they get mocking irony and if so how is it translated? Americans often don't understand British irony, understatement or humor. How would a translator convey these?

Audiences look at the translator and the speaker if both are on stage. They resemble Centre Court spectators at Wimbledon, heads swiveling in unison from left to right and back again. But it is the translator's vocalization and nonverbals that convey subtle and extra meaning. On stage, speakers have to be taught about gesturing. Translators may have also been taught but many gesticulate in order to emphasize concepts.

No wonder that presidents look at each other while translators whisper in their ears. What is being said is as important as how and when it is said. And for most, it is less worrying that things are lost in translation than what they do not want, understand or intend is gained.

Gap years for grown-ups

Young people in many countries have a socially acceptable and sanctioned period in which they are allowed and encouraged to "find themselves", "grow up", and "experience life". It is a sort of *psychological moratorium* in which the responsibilities and drudgeries of adulthood are postponed.

The privileged Victorians and Edwardians had the Grand Tour. Australasians have the Big OE (overseas experience) while the young Britons have a *gap year*. Note the quite different emphasis between OE and gap: the former positive, exciting, active; the latter slightly negative and passive.

There are in fact national schemes such as the *Peace Corps* or the *Voluntary Service Overseas* which provide well-planned, supported, and altruistic gap-year experiences. These young ambassadors are supposedly beneficial all round: for their hosts, themselves, and their nation. What is kept relatively quiet is the fact that the repatriation rate is quite high, despite all the thoughtful mixing and matching the temperament and ability of the young person and the demands of the situation.

There is some debate about the virtues of the gap year in and of itself or, indeed, if done, what best to do. Those who never had a gap year seldom regret it. Many who drifted about in an unplanned, unproductive, and unadventurous way often regretted wasting precious time. Others had the experience of their young lives and were deeply marked by what they saw and did, and where they went.

There is of course a good or bad fit between the gapper and the gap. The "techno-nerd" may not enjoy being a volunteer in an injured animal sanctuary; equally the outdoor, sporty type may really enjoy teaching English and soccer in Kenya. Some young people need to be pushed and stretched and can return quite different people. Some skill, interest or talent is awakened in them.

The Bible talks of every person being given special natural talents. What it does not tell you is how to discover or indeed sharpen them. There are countless stories of people in late middle age discovering their abilities as a writer, artist, teacher, linguist. Because of the vagaries of life, they have never discovered these latent talents. Indeed, it seems many people go to their grave without their special talent blooming, even wasting it on the desert air.

The question is how and when, if ever, adults can or should have a gap year? The concept of the sabbatical, once the preserve of academics only, is now very popular. My dictionary defines the sabbatical as "leave, often with pay, granted usually every seventh year typically for rest, travel, or research". Interestingly it lists "holiday" as a synonym.

Is there any evidence that gap years for adults are beneficial either for the person or, more importantly, financially worthwhile for the organization? The answer is no, but it's not an easy question to answer scientifically. Much, no doubt, depends on what people do. The range of activities seems endless. Some round Cape Horn in a small yacht; others take up painting in southern France. Some try further education from a few short courses to the MBA. Others try to write a book. Yet others follow the old "travel broadens the mind" maxim, although it is as likely to be the behind as the mind that gets broadened.

It's not only what people do that is important but where they are in their life stage. The 42-year-old middle manager in the empty nest with 25 years of service is a very different beast than the person of the same age with young children and a wide variety of job experiences.

Certainly sabbaticals are supposed to be about refreshment, reevaluation, taking stock. Being on the career and family treadmill is all about keeping one's head down and keeping at it. The pressure (call it challenge or stress if you prefer) seems remorseless and there is little time to stand back. Even at the traumatic, decade changing, life events (that is, turning 40 or 50) there may be only time for a brief look back, often with regret.

Sabbaticals shake people up. Maybe they're meant to! People are likely to leave their job, leave their spouse, even leave the rat race (downshifting) if given a long period of reflection. Education opens up new vistas, new ideas and possibilities. In doing so one is likely to meet new people: different people with different values, outlooks, and passions. And that can be very attractive.

So the head-down, middle-aged middle manager can find the sabbatical, a longed-for break, rather disturbing. Just like being a "homeworker", one has to impose structures on a structureless day, find friends, and more importantly set one's own goals.

A good sabbatical enables one to try out new skills the present job does not require. Often in middle life people discover they can do things they thought they could not – and enjoy them. A good sabbatical is also a time to increase knowledge: general and specialist. At a time obsessed with knowledge workers and knowledge management, it's a pretty good idea to attempt to acquire some of it. A good sabbatical should allow for networking new people. It should allow people to "get around to" things they have long put on hold. Many retired people marvel at how they ever held down a job given how busy and active they are in retirement. The explanation is, of course, the tyranny of the urgent. This is doing things not in order of salience or significance but in terms of supposed urgency. Sabbatical hopefully enables one to distinguish between the trivial and the critical.

The dilemma for the organization is whether granting sabbaticals is ultimately worth it (to the shareholder). It can be costly. But then it may be more costly not to allow them, not only because certain people will not join the organization but also because people's talents are never fully exploited. Some organizations demand a "pay-back" time such that employees have to work for at least three years after the sabbatical. Not a good idea if the major result of the sabbatical is to persuade someone they are in the wrong job.

Going open plan

How do you try to persuade people at work to do something they clearly don't want or probably really need ... like sacrifice their office for an open-plan environment? You could try a rational crypto-economic argument with a hint of threat. The "survive-or-die"; "outsourcing-to-India"; "relocation-to-Iowa" arguments may work.

The other response more beloved of PR and politician types is to overemphasize supposed benefits and clearly ignore drawbacks. Further, only certain advantages are voiced.

So, what to tell those "forcibly relocated" into that new neo-lighted, cubicled, air-controlled, bright Satanic mill of the twenty-first century? The answer is of course that massively overemphasized virtue called teamwork.

Going open plan will "facilitate communication and teamwork" which, in turn, will have great benefits for productivity and thence reward. Going open plan then somehow opens up blocked channels, frees the uncommunicative, the inhibited, and leads (quite magically) to all those glorious team-work values of trust, interdependence, and synergy.

Oh yes? More evidence-free propaganda! Given options, almost nobody wants to go open plan. If they are forced to they "cubicalize", protect themselves by erecting barriers as high as possible thus recreating their offices (about a fifth of the size). They personalize and privatize these pathetic places with all the acceptable bric-a-brac of office territoriality markers – photo of the kids, trivial awards, assorted knick-knacks the spouse won't have in the home.

It takes time to get used to the new noise level. And the fact you now have no control over the light or temperature which appears to suit no one. In fact you have now less control over all aspects of your working environment. You are in a quarter of the space with no ability to modify the environment. No wonder it is resisted almost universally.

The location change always has dramatic effects. The most profound of these is to alter friendships. The single best predictor of friendship at work is not age and stage, gender or rank, religion or values, personality or ability. It's propinquity – literally how physically close you are – and hence bump into one another. The more often you see/chat to people, the more opportunity to start up a friendship.

Move office and you move people. Almost always people make, and inevitably lose, friendships. The former is almost always interesting. It is true that people begin to talk more to others they previously said little to. But that also happens if you move from one closed-plan building to another or change the shape or even the furniture in the recreation rooms – kitchen, canteen, common room.

Shaking up relationships should not be mistaken for improved communication. It all depends on what people communicate about. Usually it is about how much they hate open plan and that the only reason for the move is cost saving. To facilitate disgruntlement is hardly the aim of the exercise.

One of the curious anomalies of the big open-plan office lies in the corners. Frequently the senior managers – the "grown-ups" are somehow excused the necessity of open plan. They have glass-fronted but still closed offices. They don't lose their space although they do their privacy. There may also be meeting rooms that are enclosed – and as a result very frequently used.

The high yield question is why these exceptions? The answer is usually privacy or perhaps quietness to facilitate concentration. Precisely. So, these things are less important for those in the cubicles?

The design of working space should be primarily determined by task. What sort of work are people doing? Equally what sort of individuals are they? We know a lot about the psychology of distraction. Noise, music, background sounds, moving objects all have a distracting effect. And they distract some individuals more than others.

The disaster scenario is the introvert trying to do a complex, intellectual task in the presence of loud, familiar, vocal music. Some tasks require serious concentration. Others are helped by distraction. People doing tedious jobs – on a conveyor belt or machine-minding – find that background music helps to keep up their mood and concentration. The time seems to pass more happily.

But increase the complexity of the task and you need a very different environment. Some highly complex tasks are done in open spaces. Air traffic control, the "bridge" of a battle ship, and so on, are open plan. But they are cool, darkish, quiet places. Close proximity to others means immediate and effective communication but strict rules govern interaction.

People are de-officed and en-cubicled by most organizations for one reason only – cost saving. Sometimes it has no long-term deleterious effect on morale or productivity. Indeed it can enhance it. But that is a function of how the offices were used beforehand and the nature of the task.

Lawyers have been moved into open plan with very mixed results. So have journalists – but most are on-the-go so it does not matter too much. Not too many accountants and actuaries are found in open plan, nor for that matter academics. And how interesting that open-plan enthusiasm is directly related to high-rent, little-space, inner city buildings. It is a triumph of spin that planners are able to sell increased crowding, more distraction and less privacy as a positive move to increase communication!

But tasks change as jobs change. And it may be that jobs that were done open plan now benefit from a move to closed. It's not, or should not, be one-way traffic.

Beware the open-plan enthusiast. They are probably a cost-cutter in disguise. First consult a serious ergonomist before you deal with planners.

Growing pains

Even swashbuckling, entrepreneurial wunderkind consultancies enter into periods of maturity. It is not as if they run out of energy or become more reflective; rather they just become larger.

The dynamics of organizations change dramatically with magnitudes of scale. Just as families change with every new addition (and death), so the psychological processes at work change as organizations grow.

Growth is usually associated with success. You aim to grow the business and conquer the world. Ever upward and onward to new heights. Maximize economies of scale, exploit sluggish competitors, increase market share.

But there is a downside, and a pretty serious one at that. It is difficult to know when this occurs – perhaps when numbers go over 50 or 100, or when the business splits sites into three or more. There are, it seems, five quite different negative consequences.

The first is the most notorious. The development of rules to ensure standardization. Yes, we have the start of *bureaucracy*. Weber, who invented the term and approached the idea, noted that all bureaucracies become more rule-bound over time. Rules, like rabbits, multiply. Unlike rabbits, they never die; never get recinded. It is ten times easier to pass rules than to abolish them.

There are two implications as organizations get bigger and older (those two things tend to go together). First, the number of rules increases exponentially. They can be the pondweed that chokes the pond, depriving it of oxygen and sunlight. Usually there seems to be a good, reasonable business case for introducing the rules, but soon they seem to inhibit innovation, block creativity, stifle imagination.

The second implication of the development of bureaucracy is learning how to "cheat the system". Innovators, change makers, cage rattlers learn to beat the system to get things done quickly and imaginatively. It can turn into a titanic struggle between the professional rule enforcer and the entrepreneurial rule breaker.

Beware the rule book, the professional administrator, the forces of standardization. The second consequence of both the size and the bureaucracy is the slow, even imperceptible movement from hetero to *homogeneity*. What this means is simply that people become more alike. They get to believe in the same things, share particular preferences, and even begin to articulate similar values. And so we have corporate culture: a set of often unstated assumptions about good and bad, right and wrong, desirable and undesirable.

It's a lot easier to be around people who share the same beliefs, instincts, and behaviors. Hence the problems of enforced diversity. There are clear advantages to heterogeneity, particularly in times of change, but like pearls that originate in pain so the move from homo- to heterogeneity seems unnatural and enforced.

Homogenous organizations tend to have strong cultures which in turn lead to that most dangerous of all phenomena – "group think", particularly by the "grown-ups". This is the explicit and implicit pressure to think and act alike in problem solving, which compromises the outcomes.

The third consequence is the emergence of *non-core jobs*, which in effect tax the organization. All business organizations, from airlines to accountancy firms, widget makers to web designers, have people with expertise to do specific tasks. They may or not be trained but have specialist jobs.

But as organizations grow, so do roles and jobs, which seem to make less (often no) substantive growth to the profits of an organization. Freeloaders may be everywhere, from "Manager Special Projects" to "Editor In-House Magazine". The real workers support them until the ratio of the real (front-line, production) workers to the overhead tips the organization into the red.

The fourth consequence is the frequency, style, and preferred medium of *communication*. Daily face-to-face contact is natural for people. Getting your nonverbals and your verbals while having a bit of banter and breeze-shooting helps you to get to know your colleagues and what they are really thinking.

Enough has been said about the problems of email, which can be cold, intrusive, easily open to misinterpretation. As organizations grow and people grow physically apart, they can drift psychologically apart as a result of the difficulties of communication.

Clarity can turn into Chinese whispers; subtlety to sarcasm. Freeloaders seem to send out endless memos, while the board goes silent. "Awaydays" have to be arranged at some expense simply to encourage chat. Newsletters have to be started so that people know what is going on. And then the little people become paranoid about the grown-ups having special secrets about the organization which they are not prepared to share.

When climate surveys show that communication is your number one problem, you know you have arrived.

The final consequence is what psychiatrists might call identity confusion disorder. People identify with their organization. Most are happy and proud to work there. Things about the organization "rub off" onto them and help shape their identity.

But in big organizations people tend to identify with their department more than the organization. Workers feel they are from accounts or engineering or marketing rather than Acme International. And their loyalty changes subtly.

As organizations get bigger and older there is it seems an inevitable, inexorable, and inescapable drive to bureaucracy, homogeneity, non-core jobs, communications problems, and identity confusion.

These are significant issues that place demands on management attention at the same time as they are managing the underlying business growth and diversification. No wonder some organizations move from growth to maturity (briefly) and thence into decline.

Happy holidays

The television nowadays appears to portray holidays in one of two very different guises: holidays in paradise and holidays from hell. This may be because there are a surprising number of people who do not like, or perhaps do not dare, to take their annual holiday entitlement. Holidays for them are punishment not reward, frustrating not fun, exhausting not refreshing.

The holiday phobic may well be in the minority and certainly more likely to be white collar. There are many who live for their two weeks in the sun, which in Europe are now more likely to be taken twice a year.

Holidays from work remain a topic of hot contention. How many weeks should a person have? Is it better and psychologically more healthy to take many shorter (that is, long weekend) breaks or to take, say, two two-week chunks? Are, or should, extra holidays be a perk of seniority or length of service? Are long holiday allowances an effective way to recruit and retain good staff? Are people prepared to trade off salary for longer holidays? Should people be compelled to take all their holidays, even if they don't want to? Should sick leave be deducted from holiday entitlement?

And what about the new trend of trading holidays as one trades air-miles? People buy and sell their holidays to their employers or other employees. There is thus a within-company, free market for holidays, which may be very desirable for many, although it has obvious health implications for those who sell all the time they have.

Puritanical Americans seem to believe that two weeks a year is sufficient; even for Europeans working in their continental offices. The Germans on the other hand have come to think that five weeks is barely enough to enjoy a proper break and experience recreation, rejuvenation, and renewal.

The self-employed know the real costs of holidays: twice the expense and nil income. Talk – or is that listen – to any London cabbie. Consultants often have the concept of a "fee earning day" and many are set targets such as 220 or 240 per year. The rest is for preparation, selling, and holidays, although there is little distinction between them from the employer's point of view.

But are there private vs public sector differences in attitudes and beliefs about holidays? Some envious people see the public sector as having many more holidays than they do. And they also note the difference in absenteeism figures suggesting public sector employees work fewer days.

Figures are not always easy to acquire but they suggest relatively small differences in entitlement between the public and private sectors. It seems public sector employees have slightly greater basic holiday entitlement but that there are no consistent patterns across various organizations – no doubt due to labor union agreement history and other factors.

In the UK, a report commissioned in 2003 by the Prison Service Pay Review Body found that senior prison officers got 25 days a year and their private sector equivalents 20 days on average. However, as seniority "clicked in" the difference did get wider with a difference of up to a third.

And an HM Treasury Report dated 2002 found little difference, with 25 days being the most common in both sectors. It did note that the public sector gave more generous parental leave; and a three-day difference in average absenteeism (7.3 private sector, 10.2 public sector).

But how desirable are holidays? It is not uncommon to meet people who never take their full leave.

Some lament their holidaylessness; others take a Protestant work ethic delight in their boastful self-denial. Many knowingly forsake taking time off which is their statutory right. Why? The answers are varied: I have no money and am saving up; I have no one to go with (attention seeking device); It is too stressful being on holiday with young children (refreshing honesty). As Noel Coward said, "Work is more fun than fun".

But people also say they are too worried about missing something at work (announcement of the redundancy package; the move to Swindon plan; the appointment of a new boss). Some also find that going on holiday means that the work piles up in their absence. Afterward there is so much to do in such a short time that the benefits of the holiday are not only canceled but the extra stress is simply not worth it. The game is not worth the candle.

Where your heart is, there is your treasure also. This applies to work most poignantly. The work–life balance brigade often seem to stress "life" over work. Yet some people (read men) find work the most fulfilling place to be. Their work gives them purpose, power, structure, and many rewards. Holidays are a distraction.

How much holiday people want and believe is good for them depends on many factors. It partly depends on what they do. Those in poorly paid, menial work over which they have little control and with which they identify little are unlikely to forsake their holidays. They literally *"come alive"* after work and when on holiday. Even without much money they take their full leave and only feel authentic when they do. The factory worker, the lowly health service employee, the traffic control policeman, the street cleaner, maximize their time off work in one guise or another.

Equally, family men or women might want to spend every moment with their children, whether it is pottering around at home or going away. Much depends on where people are in the " family cycle": this can determine whether they take and how they spend their holidays. The empty nester and the hopeful first-time buyer will have very different holidays.

Holiday entitlement is often related to service or seniority. One earns time off by commitment or stress.

But we know that younger people need more time off with their young families than older people. And we know that, despite the publicity, jobs at the bottom of organizations are more stressful than those at the top. Perhaps, paradoxically, holidays should be inversely related to seniority and service ... as one climbed the greasy pole one would have fewer holidays.

But there are also the time poor/cash rich who believe they have no time to take holidays. Some are simply sad workaholics who fear holidays. Others believe that the cost is too high and they have a unique period in their lives to make a great deal of money. Holidays are put on hold. Extra holidays are not a perk but a punishment – unless they can be saved up over the years to mean a big bonus before retirement.

Corporate and personal "away-days" to the events of the season and summer company "jollies"; "Sell in May and go away"; the apparent closure of the entire City of London for the school holidays; afternoons or days off to attend school sports days and end-of-term events ... the list is endless and endlessly frustrating for customers, suppliers, and the holiday skeptical alike.

Implicit learning and tacit knowledge

Can you learn a foreign language while asleep? Alas not. Is the best way to learn by being taught using traditional methods? Probably. But can you acquire knowledge and skills nonconsciously and be unaware of what actual knowledge has been acquired? Well, it seems so.

For many reasons researchers have become fascinated by implicit learning: perhaps the primary learning process in organizations. *First*, it is context-bound. It applies to the situation in which you (not knowingly) learned it. *Second*, the knowledge acquired through implicit learning is less manipulable by others. *Third*, it is characterized by a (natural) strong sense of intuition. *Finally*, the learning is robust over time and not susceptible to distraction.

So people acquire tacit (rather than explicit) knowledge through the implicit learning process. And how does implicit learning operate at work? There are a number of things (content areas) one has to learn at work. In rank order these are probably:

1. Performance proficiency: Essentially, how to be effective and efficient on the job.
2. Organizational goals and values: What the organization (really) strives for, rewards, and punishes.
3. Language and terminology: Learning the local jargon, acronyms, and typology talk.
4. People: How to get along with (charm, cajole, intimidate) people up and down (and across) the structure.
5. Politics: Who has the real power, how they got it, and how they keep it.
6. History: The real as well as romanticized history of the past of the workgroup and the organization as a whole.

Surprisingly perhaps, most of this knowledge is picked up incidentally. Learning comes from watching and listening rather than formal instruction. This certainly is the case when working in a foreign culture.

One of the most expensive but effective knowledge-acquisition methods is the old apprenticeship model. It is still used today for PhD students and in the arts. Hence the revival of interest in the master class.

The idea is that the master chooses his apprentice on the basis of ability/fit. Then the apprentice shadows his/her master for many years, doing at first menial tasks and observations but gradually followed by more and more complex tasks. The master hands over his/her knowledge, skill, and wisdom. Indeed it is this long line of followers or devotees that determines a master's longevity.

Most organizations have all the modern HR-driven accoutrements of formal learning. There are induction courses for new members, mentors for some, coaches for others. There are training courses and in-house mini MBAs. Many organizations proudly call themselves learning organizations and some even try to take that concept seriously.

But you don't have to be a cynic to see the yawning gap between the explicit and the implicit; the mission statement and the management practices; the much propounded values and the real behaviors behind.

Few organizations try to describe their culture: that fuzzy mix of values, norms, and practices that together pre- and proscribe how employees should behave. You sort of "pick it up" from what you see and hear. Despite what the blurb says, this is how things are done "round here".

Implicit knowledge acquisition is about perceptiveness. It's about picking up the small cues that are all important in business life. Successful people learn to read the signs. The corporate-culturally-dyslexic become marginalized.

The hard bit is the doublespeak. It's learning a secret code. Just as reference writers and readers learn to encode and decode information about individuals, so in organizations employees have to understand the difference between what is said and what is meant.

Thus "challenge" means stress. "New challenges" mean more stress. What organizations choose to, and can, measure says a lot about them. Measure checking-in and you value presentism. Measure customer feedback and the forms become ultimately important. Time (deadlines, schedules, targets) is easy to measure as is money. But quality and quantity of performance are not. Hence you learn what's important to the organization by noting what is measured, by whom, and when.

Anthropologists learn about a culture by joining it. They learn from small samples of behavior how to be a real, accepted member of the tribe. There are no etiquette books, nor old hands explaining the history, meaning, and function of social rituals. But they learn implicitly how to fit in. In this sense, all employees are anthropologists when it comes to understanding corporate culture.

Leadership fundamentals

The fundamental characteristics of the human species have powerful implications for the nature of leadership at work. And you don't have to be a pseudo or crypto sociobiologist (from Venus or Mars) to accept the points.

First, we are social animals: we live in groups. We need/like/prefer the company of others. We like to be included and fear exclusion. We punish with ostracism, with solitary confinement, with abolition to the ends of the earth.

But, being social animals, we need to learn from a very early age *to get along with others*. Adults have to go to social skills training or emotional intelligence facilitation classes. Those who somehow did not pick up the knowhow of getting along have to go to remedial classes.

Social skills are about perception, charm, flexibility. They are about reading others, amusing them, and being aware of how one is coming across. They are about "reading the signals" that others emit verbally, vocally and visually. They are about thoughts and emotions. The EQ movement put emphasis on being able to understand *and* manage your own and others' emotions.

Leaders need social skills. They need to be attractive to others; to be able to persuade and charm them. They need to be comfortable around others. More, they need to know how to get along with others who are different from themselves; older and younger, with different education and ethnic backgrounds, friends and enemies.

Some leaders have few social skills. But they never last in the media-sensitive, free market economies. They tend only to be found in corrupt or bureaucratic countries and organizations where politics, force, and power determine abilities rather than market forces or the democratic forces of all stakeholders.

Getting along with others starts to be learned in kindergarten. As does the second fundamental skill: getting *ahead* of others. Every social group has a status hierarchy. This can be seen in the toddler playground as easily as it can be observed in the boardroom. Some people learn to get ahead: to be among the chosen, to command respect, to be listened to. How many leaders have been valedictorian/head prefect? And in a school where they have been elected by the scholars, not the teachers: a subtle but important difference.

Every organization – however seemingly opposed to the idea – has its status hierarchy. The cabinet has "First Among Equals"; monasteries have abbots; orchestras have conductors.

Leaders are chosen on many factors: their ability, charisma, believability, articulacy. You get ahead in different groups through possessing different factors. One "competency" to be Archbishop of Canterbury is "holiness", a characteristic somewhat specific to that job.

Leaders have to learn to exploit their talents: to be likeable, electable, and therefore powerful. There is a skill to getting ahead and another to staying ahead. Apart from the Stalinist method of actually exterminating the opposition, any aspirant leader needs to know how to get ahead.

The third feature all social groups have is a *belief system*. They are "religions" of a sort and they fulfil various functions, primarily to give meaning to the capriciousness of life. All ideologies serve a purpose. The more successful the ideology/religion, the more it speaks to the deep and fundamental yearnings of human beings. People need a positive identity, a good story of their past, a sense of mission, and so on.

Equally, at work, people need pride in their product, their company, their achievement, and their history. It is the job of a leader to tell a good story; to make the past a glorious struggle and the future a certain journey.

There is a difference between spin and ideology; between PR and a belief system. The former are fickle and cynical; the latter are coherent and usually believable.

Leaders need more than a story, a good line, or a hopeful message. They need an ideology for their times, their people, and their circumstance. Hence all the Mission–Vision rhubarb of recent business gurus. It seems leaders had forgotten this aspect of their stewardship: the "meaning–making" function.

Often the circumstances dictate the appropriateness of the ideology. Today it's called situational leadership. But there are also enduring themes to all ideologies: justice, honour, equity, and so on.

People die for their beliefs: a fact manifest from the earliest times to today's suicide bombers. People will endure great hardship and deprivation for a belief system.

Good leaders know how to exploit, explain, and explore beliefs. A great leader gets an "ism" if they are lucky. Hence, Thatcherism, Fordism, and so on. Their beliefs are coherent, timely, and communicated with power and conviction.

Good leaders need to *spot trends*. Trends in the market, in consumer tastes, in workforce skills. They need to get ahead of the game both within and outside the organization. They need to be good at their own succession planning to blaze the trail.

And they need to be able to *engage others* at various points on their way to the top. They need charm, social skills, emotional intelligence, interpersonal sensitivity: whatever it is currently called. It means getting people on-side, fired up, behind you in good times and bad.

So you want to be a business leader? Here is the test: what is the evidence that you have and can and will *get along with* others (all others) you need to deal with at work; *get ahead* of the pack including other board directors, competitors, and the press; espouse a *timely, coherent ideology* relevant to the company, the product, and the employees?

Leading from the heights

In that memorable and very British television sketch of the early 1960s, Cleese, Barker, and Corbett explained and portrayed the British class system. Tall, ectomorphic, Cambridge graduate John Cleese looks down his nose at respectable, bespectacled, endomorphic Ronnie Barker. Both look down on the chirpy, vertically challenged, but perfectly formed Ronnie Corbett who "knows his place".

Was the height difference metaphoric or factual? Research confirms what many suspect but dare not articulate: tall people tend to be more successful in life.

A recent study in the prestigious *Journal of Applied Psychology* by two American professors (Tim Judge and Daniel Cable) reported some extremely interesting results. They analysed four sets of data collected in both Britain and America that followed over 8000 people through adolescence to working adults. It recorded their height, weight, chosen job, their salary, and so on.

 Once weight, gender, and age were controlled for, there was a clear, significant positive correlation between income and height. It is important to control for these three factors as men tend to be about five inches taller than women; people lose one to three inches in height over their lifetime; and heavier people tend to be taller.

To be precise, every inch in height was worth $789 in pay or about £500. An individual who is 72 inches tall could be expected to earn $5525 more per year than someone 65 inches tall. And if you could add this up over a lifetime of, say, 30 years this amounts to $166,000.

Interestingly height was related to income in all jobs: blue and white collar, service and sales, crafts and clerical, management and nonmanagement. However the correlation was strongest in those jobs that required more contact with customers. And it was stronger in men than women.

Height was correlated with both objective and subjective measures of performance – even in accounting and computer programming. Taller people are better then? If so – why?

There are many possible answers. Height is associated with good childhood nutrition, which is associated with health, intelligence, and height. One is stunted by childhood neglect, trauma, and poverty. They could all have an effect.

A second explanation is about confidence. Taller people tend to have greater self-esteem and self-confidence than shorter people. This confidence helps them to be more successful and achieve higher social status. Tall people are, or seem, more authoritative, assertive, leader-like, stronger. Height predicts social esteem which predicts both performance and leader emergence.

Evolutionary theorists can also wade in with explanations. Big (equals tall, heavy, strong) men had evolutionary advantage. They had strength and power and could protect others. Tall males are alpha males.

Height as a virtue is enshrined in our language: you "walk tall"; people "look up" to you; you strive to be "high and mighty".

No doubt studies such as this elicit three reactions. The *first* and most primitive is denial. This attempts to deny the validity of all these studies by showing them to be fundamentally flawed. The *second* is to call for lawyers, legislation, and all the apparatus of discrimination to ensure every workplace has a normal distribution in height. This of course could lead to economic and competitive disadvantage but this is rarely a concern of the anti-discrimination lobby.

A *third* equally bizarre response may be to have height education in schools that attempts both to confront heightism and give special self-esteem tuition to those below average.

Some people who are different have found great wells of motivation in their desire to compensate for that difficulty. And, let's be frank, you need more than self-confidence and height to get on in life – except perhaps as a basketball player.

Learning from mistakes

We all make serious selection mistakes. The divorce statistics alone are testimony to the fact that despite the investment of considerable time, effort, and money, we get it wrong. We select where we should reject and vice versa. Of course we know only about the former and not the latter.

Most can recall that charming, seemingly talented and motivated candidate who somehow transformed into a surly, ineffective, and lazy employee. Why do supposedly well-educated, sparkling, and emotionally intelligent people suddenly seem dim-witted, gauche, wet squibs? Whence the metamorphosis? Or did we just miss a trick?

Selection interviews are often an elaborate charade. A hall of mirrors where nothing is what it seems. Neither side is strictly honest. Only certain things can be asked. Only certain answers are given.

There is now a lethal trio of factors that seem to inhibit interviewers doing a good job: preventing them being perceptive, psychologically minded and, as a result, making a good decision. The first is simple *lack of training and insight:* which questions to ask, when – and how to interpret the often ambiguous feedback. Good interviewers have "the third eye", insight, perceptiveness, call it what you will. The second factor is *political correctness* and its close cousin – legitimate litigation fear. Ask the unacceptable question about demography (age, family), beliefs, or background and you are snookered. Employment lawyers are waiting in the wings. The third is the candidate's *skills and experience in dissimulation*, which means their ability to present the "truth" selectively.

No wonder the chosen individual turns out somewhat differently than was expected.

But organizations that try to prevent making the same errors again invest some effort in going back and reviewing what they missed. The assumption is there are clues that were ignored, warning signs overlooked, and incorrect assumptions made. Further, what many discover, if they examine a whole "batch" of failures, derailers, and deceivers, is that there seem to be common factors among them. These can end up being a rather useful inventory of warning signs.

So what are these warning signs? There are at least half a dozen. To find out about them takes careful questioning of the individuals and those that know them well. Almost by definition the problematic employee cannot or will not divulge the truth on these issues. Also both too much or too little of the same thing can be a problem. Consider, for instance, self-esteem. People with *low self-esteem* tend to be underachievers and have feelings of worthlessness. They rarely exploit their talents because of their low confidence. They rarely get selected, but their opposites do. Those with overbearing, *inflated self-esteem* are at best supremely self-confident and at worst deeply arrogant. They feel special, above others, deserving of special treatment and praise. They may be indifferent to others, haughty, and quite unbearable. At the interview this all comes over as confidence; on the job as arrogance and narcissism. Low self-esteem is manifest in feelings of worthlessness but its opposite is grandiose, glory seeking and recognition hunger.

A second theme is what one might call *sensitivity*. Difficult employees are moody, brittle, quick to take slights. They are the opposite of robust. They do not deal with setbacks well. It is the worst of combinations. They suffer stress easily and have few good coping mechanisms. These people can be supra-sensitive and even paranoid.

Third, is a surprising *immaturity*. This is manifest by egocentrism and self-indulgence. These people do not do postponement of gratification. They must have everything now. They lack all those old-fashioned virtues like control and responsibility. They are easily bored, fickle, demanding; childlike in the pejorative sense of the word.

The fourth issue, and this is a big one, is *problems with relationships*. Again, as above, these can take many and varied forms. They may be excessively dependent or independent; they may be overly respectful of authority or deeply anti-authoritarian in their beliefs and behaviors. Some people are cold fish; a bit of a loner. Others really do find the idea of solitary confinement a torture and can't be alone at all. They need support, reassurance all the time. Or they may be shy or inadequate and seem to have few close friends or interest in social activities.

A fifth factor is about *morality* ... and it is pretty important. It is more than being honest and ethical. It's about being manipulative and callous. It can be expressed as carelessness or casualness; of simply not caring. Often there is a shocking, even impressive ability to excuse, justify, and explain away any course of action. These people believe rules, regulations, and codes of behavior do not apply to them. They can rely on their seductive, persuasive charm to get them out of tricky spots they personally get into. They don't do ethics, morality, and so on, and have clever ways of sophistry and casuistry to explain away their behavior.

A final factor is a pervasive sense of *negativity and pessimism*. This may be manifest as an obsession with failures in the past and being resentful. It may also be expressed as rigidity. These people have a great memory for slights from the past and a sense of fatalism. Que sera, sera. They can be overcautious.

Beware also those who seem enigmatic, somehow intangible or, worse than that, overstep boundaries, even at the interview. Often, as always, there are clues in the past: upbringing, schooling, early job history. Childhood instability, a history of seeking counseling, academic failure, and frequent, often dramatic, changes in lifestyle all add up to potential trouble.

Of course, candidates are eager to hide, and possibly experienced in covering up, information that falls into one of the above categories. But seeing through them is the skill of the perceptive interviewer. And given how legally difficult and expensive it is to get rid of people these days, the payoff in making better selection decisions may be well worth the investment in examining these warning signs.

The lessons of experience

How do you make young people appreciate how the world works? Despite, or perhaps as a result of, their education they can be at once arrogant and ignorant, demanding and complying, dependent and independent. What's the best introduction to reality for a 20 year old?

For many an "old buffer" the answer would be a stint in the army. But they were and are fundamentally wrong. The world is in fact very unmilitary. And it has been estimated that up to a third of "rough sleepers" in London have had army experience. Conscripts to armies tell you they learn work avoidance, bureaucratic management, and buck-passing – hardly desirable attitudes. It may be different for volunteers, but the jury is out.

The paper route, the job at McDonald's, and the Saturday job in the hairdresser's or hardware store are better. But it could be argued that being a waiter/waitress in an undermanned environment (that is, short-staffed) is the best introduction to the world of work.

You have to deal with irascible, capricious, demanding, unempathic customers who, you are told, pay your salary. The skills required to deal with such a task are manifold. You have to learn to charm and to negotiate, to be assertive and insightful. You need to be adaptable and resourceful, as well as tough and resilient.

You also have to be multiskilled. You may have to calculate the bill, wipe up some scrambled egg, pick up some fresh vegetables, be familiar with the menu, or placate the guests. It does not matter that you have not done any of it before or have never been shown how to do it. There isn't anyone else. This is very different from simply pouring shots behind the bar, however busy or rowdy and demanding the customers.

Good life lessons can also be gained from being in sales for a period. The great insight to be learned here is that effort and ability are directly related to outcome. Low base pay but good commission is a sobering experience.

You learn to cope with rejection (again and again); to be resilient and optimistic. You learn how to read others and persuade them to do things they would otherwise not. You learn how to be adaptable and hard-working. You learn how to pace yourself.

But ultimately there is nothing like starting your own business, however small. Read the hagiographic obituaries of multimillionaires and you find they were running things in the ninth grade. Some mowed lawns, others baked cakes, some washed cars. The clever ones soon begged to employ their friends and take a good cut.

Being an entrepreneur, however modest, teaches you about markets and competition. It is a crash program in economic forces, supply and demand, even how to motivate staff. Studies of young African children who look after their parents' fruit stall while they are away show them to be considerably advanced in terms of applied arithmetic, consumer understanding, and insights into human nature compared to Western children at top private schools.

An entrepreneur learns about cash flow, investment in new products, what to do with old stock. No wonder then that top management consultants look for evidence of entrepreneurship in applicants, even in undergraduates. Management experience is good – entrepreneurship even better. It's more proactive, more challenging. It's about the creation of money.

Most of our politicians seem to be lawyers or teachers. Far fewer have evidence of entrepreneurship in their résumés. It is quite one thing to be dedicated to the equitable distribution of money and yet another to be interested in wealth creation. Better to be equally poor or equitably rich? Certainly it may do ideological wealth distributors no harm to have some experience of running their own businesses.

Mrs Thatcher was a product of the mercantile class. Its values drove her: thrift, the work ethic, obeying the law. So you may gain the benefits of entrepreneurship by observing it closely as a child. But too many children of too successful entrepreneurs end up spoiled, indulgent types with little sense of their privilege. Hence the short-term rise and fall of mini-empires.

The moral of the story is this. Early exposure to the world of work shapes people. They seek out and are shaped by part-time work experiences that later in part determine the jobs they select and are selected for. And the best way to learn about the slings and arrows of misfortune is running your own show, however modest.

Lies, self-love, and paranoia

Recent research compared the personalities of inmates of a maximum security prison and successful CEOs of quoted companies. The game, of course, was to find similarities rather than differences. And this is indeed what was found. The groups are most similar on three personality disorders: antisocial, narcissistic, and paranoid.

And this partly explains why such "unusual" types make it to, and fall from, the very top. The problem is that sheer ability and hard work alone are not enough to climb the slippery pole to the top of organizations. And it is more than opportunistically exploiting one's luck, marrying the boss's daughter, or getting a PR expert to manage your reputation.

It is no accident that paranoid, narcissistic psychopaths often succeed in life. If an individual is bright and good looking, having the above personality disorder may be just the ticket to (short-term) business success ... and subsequent disaster for all concerned.

There have been various fascinating studies in this relatively new area of *organizational psychiatry*. By far the most commonly studied is the psychopath, sometimes called sociopath, antisocial personality, or mischievous personality.

Psychopaths tend to be superficial, grandiose, manipulative, and totally lacking in empathy, long-term goals, or remorse. They are impulsive and irresponsible. These managers show a disregard for, and violation of, the rights of others. They often have a history of being difficult, delinquent, or dangerous. They show a failure to conform to social norms, for example with respect to lawful behaviors (repeatedly performing acts that are grounds for arrest, imprisonment, and serious detention). These include lying, stealing, and cheating. Psychopaths are always deceitful, as indicated by repeated lying, use of aliases, or conning others for personal profit or pleasure. They can be nasty, aggressive, con artists – the sort who are profiled on business crime programs. They are massively impulsive and fail to plan ahead. They live only in, and for, the present.

Psychopaths show irritability and aggressiveness, as indicated by repeated physical fights or assaults. They can't seem to keep still – ever. They manifest a terrifying, reckless disregard for the physical and psychological safety of self and others – or the business in general. They are famous for being consistently irresponsible. Repeated failure to sustain consistent work behavior or to honor financial obligations are their hallmark. Most frustrating of all, they show lack of remorse. They are indifferent to, or afterward rationalize, hurting, mistreating, or stealing from another. They never learn from their mistakes. It can seem that labeling them as antisocial is a serious understatement.

Through bluff, lies, and manipulation, psychopaths, perhaps surprisingly, can succeed in business, particularly fast-growing, poorly regulated businesses, or those in crisis. Detailed studies of industrial psychopaths have shown that they tend to adopt particular strategies. First, they build networks of one-to-one relationships with powerful individuals, but they (and other co-workers) are soon abandoned if not useful. Detractors and critics are systematically "neutralized" by raising doubts about their competence and motives. They desperately try to stop co-workers sharing information about them. They avoid meetings because of maintaining their multiple façades. They work on their impressive ability to deceive even the most sophisticated and hard-bitten manager.

A second, very dangerous group of characters are the narcissists, in love with themselves. They communicate nothing but confidence, which in confusing times can be very attractive to both employers and shareholders. But their self-love soon derails themselves and their companies.

Narcissism is essentially a disorder of self-esteem. They behave as if they are the most important person in the organization (and world) and that *everyone* should recognize their special place. Most eventually self-destruct because their grandiosity and self-preoccupation blind their better judgement and business perspective. (So there is a God!)

Narcissists can't bear criticism however mild or helpful. Rage, tantrums, tears may result or deep shame and hurt quite out of proportion to the critical feedback.

So they become selfish, demanding, and manipulative. They rarely seek help for their problem until there is a crisis. In a curious way they may be seen as natural products of the "me" generation. In this sense pathology is only a heightened version of normality. And, in some pathological organizations it may be that being a narcissist represents the best way of coping with the demands and tensions of modern multinationals. Indeed, in the performing arts, in the fashion business, and in the media, it sometimes seems as if narcissism is a course requirement!

And if your boss is a narcissist? Do a lot of accept, admire, and respect. Pay a lot of attention but don't get too close. Don't expect too much in return. Be very gentle with upward feedback.

Finally, there are the paranoid. In some sectors, their suspicion seems both normal and even desirable. They are distrustful and suspicious of others at work. The motives of colleagues and bosses are interpreted as malevolent, all the time. The "enemy" is both without and within. Paranoids suspect, without much evidence, that others are exploiting, harming, or deceiving them about almost everything, both at work and at home. They are preoccupied with unjustified doubts about the loyalty or trustworthiness of subordinates, customers, bosses, shareholders, and so on, on both big and small matters. They are reluctant to confide in others (peers at work) because of their fear that the information will be used against them, kept on file, or used to sack them. They may even be wary of using email.

They read hidden or threatening meanings into the most benign remarks or events, from emails to coffee-room gossip, and they remember them. They are certainly hypersensitive to criticism. They persistently bear grudges against people, going back many years, and can remember even the smallest slight. They perceive attacks on their character or reputation that others don't see and are quick to react angrily or to counterattack. They seem hyper-alert and sensitive. They have recurrent suspicions, without justification, regarding the fidelity of their sexual or business partners and can be pretty obsessed with sex.

Readers of this essay will perhaps recognize and have had experience of dealing with one or more of these personality types at work. Working with them is always a problem and can sometimes prove a nightmare.

Living on: letting go

Retirement: a golden period of life as a rich reward for hard graft? Or a slow decline into obscurity before the grim reaper strikes? Is it eternal senior citizen holidays for (eternally) fit fifty-somethings, or gaga oblivion in circumstances of deteriorating health, wealth, and stealth?

There are now many types of retirement. Gone are those comforting images of the postwar era when the breadwinner collected his gold watch for long service and dedicated his (relatively few) remaining years to gardening, philately, and the grandchildren. One can retire from many things at many stages of life.

It is now not uncommon to "retire" many times, like a successful cricketer. Early retirement, downshifting, spending more time with the family, doing more voluntary work. You can retire from a job, a role, a profession, or an organization.

Traditionally, retirement means leaving work: the 9 to 5, responsibility, goals, targets, and the like. It means, with luck, that through pension schemes and company benevolence, one leaves the day-to-day grind of work life while still receiving some (modest) reward from the organization in monetary and other terms.

Retirement is a form of letting go. It involves the psychology of loss. Loss of structure, income, identity, and purpose. It is the loss of influence. It hits some more than others. Few care about leaving menial, tedious, repetitive, dangerous, or dirty jobs. Few machine-minders or traffic control police yearn for what the job provided. But there are many in jobs genuinely loved and where there is intrinsic satisfaction. Here retirement can be a sudden shock, even a slow death. It can be all the more traumatic for those CEOs, politicians, and single-minded careerists whose reason for being was what they *did*.

For successful professionals, the job often brings power and influence. They can command respect and what they say is carefully listened to. They can change lives, get media coverage – make a difference. And then, quite suddenly, they are forgotten, ignored – yesterday's people. They no longer have PAs to do everything from booking holidays to buying the spouse's birthday present. Worse, they suddenly notice the effects of aging: loss of hair and hearing, dental and visual problems, weight gain, loss of energy and fitness. The time-to-live divided by the time-since-birth fraction looks distinctly depressing.

For the unprepared, retirement can bring the shock of nothingness, oblivion, pointlessness, and can be overwhelming. Few, however, are totally unprepared, although their preparations can be rather unhelpful.

All of us want to "live on". It is one of the deepest needs of all animals aware of death. It is the "wellspring" of all religions. Even at work, people want to leave their mark. They want some monument to their memory. Those with money can endow chairs, sponsor colleges, start business schools in their name. The more modest provide small scholarships for the deserving few.

Some, like the Victorians in their faintly preposterous necropolises, want a building to their memory. Something concrete to see, to touch, to venerate. Politicians like to enact policies that stand the test of time. They also like to write their autobiographies which are their version of history, the truth as they see it, and so on.

Many worry about this legacy. And they do so justly, because they know that often in their climb to the top they have been callous, egocentric, and manipulative. They know there is a long path of envious, angry, resentful people just waiting for them to go. This near paranoia may be well placed.

The pictures of statues to Stalin, Mao, Saddam Hussein being toppled represent the abiding fear of many near-retirees. Some believe their legacy will be crushed, reversed even publicly despised by those that follow. Hence, many try preemptive measures by getting their "henchmen" (trusted colleagues) to take over and keep the light of their memory burning.

One way to cope is never quite to retire; staying on in some advisory capacity. These people may even fight for a grand, if meaningless, title. But little helps identity. Professors are desperate for emeritus status, and officers of field rank enjoy being addressed as "Colonel" in the pub. It makes them feel valued and important again. All politicians long to fade away in the upper house. Grandiose titles, a happy daily rate, no constituency requirements. Perfection. The model of retirement. A benevolent nursing home, where one has even more privileges than when properly working.

And so business has copied the model with "Chairman Emeritus", "Nonexecutive Advisor to the Board", "Vice President Business Mission", and the like.

Is retirement the responsibility of the retiree alone? The only part the organization seems to believe it has a role in, is in organizing some short (= cheap) preretirement course for those expensive senior executives they are eager to get rid of via early retirement, or voluntary severance programs.

Angry, disenfranchised, retired workers can be more than a nuisance. They can turn into whistle-blowers and "reputation terrorists". How, as well as when, people leave work is important.

Companies pay a high price both for letting people work well beyond their sell-by date as well as edging out the able, loyal, and motivated. There is life beyond work ... and abundant life at that.

Retirement is a new start: new education, new interests, new relationships. But for many, the sacrifice to work has been great and the preparation for good retirement limited or superficial. The past is another country. One can and must let go – most things – and gradually. It's better for all concerned. It is said one dies as one lived – and so it is with retirement. One slips down the greasy pole much as one climbed it.

Looking the part

Is it true that in these politically correct, litigiously obsessed, but spin-doctor, image-conscious times, physical appearance as much as ability and experience determines who is appointed? Is it survival of the handsomest? Surely no one dares differentiate between candidates on how they look – except of course in the theater, movies, and fashion where it is all important.

The job of a play's or film's casting director is as interesting as it is challenging. It is, of course, a selection job. Out of the many, many hopeful applicants for the role, those must be chosen who somehow best encapsulate the characters with their looks, voices, mannerisms, and personae. Villains have to look like villains; heroes real heroes.

The whole package needs to fit. The voice might be right, but the stature wrong. The look may be frightful and menacing but the physiology too puny to magnify the effect. And most directors want to be a little original, a little quirky. Hence the curious mixture of detective heroes on American cop-shows, from bald, lolly-pop consumers to short, square, binocularly challenged individuals.

Yet obituaries of film stars show how they tended to play similar roles. No doubt because they looked the part. Often people who knew these characters intimately reported that in effect they were quite unlike their celluloid characters. "Bad guys", characterized by gruff, monosyllabic one-liners, were often amusing raconteurs; while matinee idols off screen were selfish, loutish, and vulgar.

This is all very well in the artsy-craftsy world of drama and theatre, but what happens in business? To what extent are those who select senior managers influenced by what a manager should look like?

Academic studies on physical looks make rather depressing reading. Various well-conducted criminological studies have shown that physical features frequently sway judgments of innocence and guilt. The scared, small-eyed, heavily built, shaven-haired defendant has far less chance of being judged correctly innocent than the large-blue-eyed, neotenous cherub. Attractiveness influences both juries and judges: bail levels, fines, and jail sentences are often partly a reflection of the defendant's looks.

There are a host of other studies on physical looks that show how certain features trigger reactions. Shown pictures of the identical person wearing spectacles or not, attached to a résumé, people rate those wearing glasses as more intelligent. The effect has much less impact during interviews where voice, vocabulary, and answers to questions can overpower the simple prop of spectacles. But looks count – often subtly and very imprecisely.

Are these small invidious factors in play at work? Despite all the hype, is selection as much based on physical properties as it is on ability? One way to investigate this problem is to take 100 top executives, or better 1000, and see how they differ from population norms on their physical appearance.

Are top people taller? Are they slimmer than average? Are fewer top male executives balder than average? Using either metrics of the face (space between eyes, length of nose) or rater judgments of attractiveness – are top people different?

Or if all this smacks of too much elitism, examine social class E rather than A and see if they differ systematically from the norm.

It is not particularly easy research. Certainly we have reasonable population norms on height, weight, and the like but it is pretty important to get a good random population sample to show that any effect found is not directly related to one industry or another.

And what if we found, as many suspect, clear physical differences between people at different levels of the organization that have effectively nothing to do with the job they do? There are probably two powerful reactions to this observation.

The first is the shrill cry of unfair discrimination from the conspiracy theorists who see prejudice everywhere. There are no doubt associations of the short, the fat, and many other groups that believe they are discriminated against. Their argument is that physical characteristics play no part in how well they do the job and that they are, therefore, victims. Some would even call for height quotas and the like, ensuring that, by law, as many top executives are below the average height as above it.

Battling for the other side are the covariance theorists who point out that height and weight are in fact linked to social class, which in turn is linked to education, which is linked to skill, knowledge, and attitudes. Thus the reason why top people tend to be slimmer and taller than average is that these are covariates of education, which is indeed a good predictor of success at work.

There can be strong or weak variants of either the conspiracy or covariance theories. Thus one could try sociobiology as a strong version of covariance theorists. It might go something like this: mate selection is partly a function of physical attractiveness. Women like fit, bright, wealthy males; males like pretty, fecund women. The more you "fit the bill", the more choice of spouses you have – and vice versa. Thus certain physical types do better. Alpha males – who have trophy wives – are top of the chain. True for the mountain gorillas of Burundi; true for the management team in Baltimore.

Photos often used to accompany résumés. Selectors used to call for them. They do not dare do so now, lest they be thought of as influenced by the person's (facial) appearance. But height, body shape, skin texture, hair length and quality do make a difference – for both men and women. Indeed there are "consultants" who sell their skill on helping you maximize your assets and minimize your limitations. And the great rise of cosmetic surgery may be seen by some as a good business investment. They know that in selection, in presentations, and probably at assessments, it really does help to look the part.

A matter of confidence

Imagine that there is a very good (reliable, robust, sensitive, valid) test of a person's *real ability:* the ability to learn a language or play a musical instrument, or learn a new complex computer program – or whatever. Then consider giving the test to many thousands of people from all backgrounds.

As well as completing the test, people are asked to rate or assess their ability on this specific task. So we have data on their *actual* and *perceived* ability. This procedure can lead to the identification of three quite clear groups: the over-, the under-, and the realistically confident. Who are these people? How did they get like that? What is it like to try and train them?

The *overconfident* are perhaps the most curious. They (honestly) overrate their abilities. They believe they have attributes and qualities that the test reveals they do not. The question is the cause and consequence of this *hubris.* The overconfident are deluded – but why? Are they victims, or very happy and responsive recipients, of self-esteem programs? Are they simply naive with little self-insight in general? Have they never received accurate feedback on their abilities? All three could be true.

The self-esteem industry believes, in an evidence-free sort of way, that the "secrets of success" lie not in assessing and developing abilities, but rather in bolstering esteem. They see low self-esteem as the *cause* and not the consequence of underachievement. So that is what they work on in the sure and unshakeable faith that told enough times one can do it, one can. Perhaps. But you do need the native wit, the ability, the wherewithal to do the job.

In fact we now seem to have an overpraised generation of youngsters who have only ever had positive feedback, self-esteem training, or, perhaps, therapy. They may never have been properly assessed or tested and certainly not given feedback on their aptitudes and capacities.

The overconfident can be "difficult" in the classroom. They may react with astonishment, anger, and antagonism (in that order) to find they are somewhat less talented than they believe they are. The first response is to rubbish the teacher, the test or the technology. To maintain their self-image, some may resign or retreat, blocking out the feedback. It is all too painful.

Much depends on the importance of the skill to the self-concept of the individual. The more important; the more resistant. It also depends on the extent to which they believe (through hard work, practice, effort) they can get better or simply that what they have is their lot. Incrementalists may accept the feedback and try to improve. And (within the limits of their ability range), they might. The overconfident can seem cocky and talent-less. Their inflated opinion of themselves is rarely attractive – and is at the opposite end of the spectrum to classic British understatement.

The *underconfident* are no less deluded but they are carriers of humility rather than hubris. Of course, there is affected and real humility. Affected humility may be hubris in disguise. This strategy is favored in certain circles. People misrepresent their real belief by protestation of innocence, naiveté, ignorance, skill-lessness and the rest. It disarms others and can be a highly effective negotiation technique.

But the really underconfident genuinely incorrectly assess their potential. And, for the most part, these are self-fulfilling prophesies. Believe you can't and you can't. This is the mantra of the self-esteem guys, but what they miss is that this is true only of those with ability. It is no use telling the tone-deaf that they can sing or have fine voices, and so on, when any amount of self-belief won't work.

It is said that girls are given humility training and boys training in hubris. Any teacher will attest to the joy, even wonder, of taking a clearly talented, but underconfident student and giving them both the confidence and the will to succeed. Like a desert plant when watered, they bloom beautifully.

But some underconfident people resist the treatment, as anorexics deny the incontrovertible feedback of the mirror. Underconfidence can have deep roots and fulfil various purposes. You never fail if you never try. You are never picked on if you claim no ability. But like flowers that waste their fragrance on the desert air, they waste their talent. They can respond to self-esteem therapy, but it needs to be done very sensitively.

The third group are OK. Some know they are below average and they are; and some above average. They are realists who have probably come to an understanding of their ability or lack of it, through old-fashioned practice, effort, and feedback.

Perhaps much of the enthusiasm for the executive 360° feedback program is to try to reduce both humility and hubris. We only get a good sense of our real potential through trial and error and feedback. The video camera, like the mirror, is a powerful and disinterested trainer. It might not explain the cause of below or above expected performance, but it can portray it pretty ruthlessly.

Having, and accepting, an accurate sense of self and one's abilities is an index of mental heath and adjustment.

It is an index of how close a friend you are of reality.

Modern management styles

What happened to MBWA (Management by Walking Around) or the "One-minute manager"? Perhaps the managers who spent all their time walking around lost their way, forgot to do some planning, or did not notice the need for marketing.

And who has quality circles now? Who dresses down on Friday? Why no more process reengineering or managers called coaches? Their demise may be a source of fun to outsiders who observe them – although perhaps less amusing to those at the sharp end of silver bullet, magic potion management.

Individual managers will always do their own thing, no matter what happens to management fads. A heady mixture of personality, preferences, and pathology means that individual managers often adopt quirky styles they believe to be effective. In minor doses they are little more than amusing quirks. Taken to extreme they can lead to disaster.

Acronym Management: This is in-group abbreviation management. "Has the CFO completed his KRAs for the FRM?" The aim is to speak a private language that excludes all nonspeakers. The more you can speak the jargon, the closer you are to the center of power.

Blue-sky Management: This is theoretical, futurological, big picture management. It is not about the grubby here-and-now or the tedium of appraisals, balance sheets, or customer satisfaction. It is the magic world of business gurus. Managers believe their job is to understand the big issues and all else will follow.

Amnesic Management: This is management by forgetting, but highly selective forgetting, for example disagreement at meetings, but most of all serious promises made to others. Not to be confused with Alzheimer's Management, which is a more extreme version.

Anecdotal Management: This is story-telling, ripping-yarn, guru-parable management. Direction is given and decisions made by use of curiously repeated anecdotes of long-past events that often have seemingly nothing to do with the problems in hand.

Corporate Entertaining Management: Not only is the customer king but he or she needs a good lunch and a memorably sponsored event, frequently. The marketing budget is spent with enthusiasm by this party-going manager who loves to be at the centre of things.

Doppler-effect Management: This is achieved by walking very fast and purposefully in public places. Conversations are all sound bites about future meetings – "we must link up!" or "lunch soon!" These are said earnestly just before disappearing upstairs, down in a lift, or round the corner.

Email Management: This is noncontact management by sending continual, chevron-urgent missives, instructions, minutes, and memos. It is measured by the word, not by the impact. Curiously, follow-up on any of the bewildering babble to emerge from the fingertips of these shy managers seems unimportant.

PA Management: This is management by having a bossy secretary do all the (dirty) work. She (for it always is) is usually a mixture of Attila the Hun and Carry On Matron. Often the PA is the power behind the throne.

Personal Development Management: This is management by degrees; by studying; by the organization paying for the manager to complete a very expensive MBA. Managers are frequently on courses, completing assignments or on fact-finding missions. Good for their career, bad for the business.

Peer Meeting Management: This is management by talking to other managers in and outside the business – literally. This is supposed to reduce the SILO problem, ensure better integration, and improve communication. Equally meeting managers from other similar businesses (size, sector) in nice hotels in the (ideally foreign) country is even better for gossip and a free lunch.

Reorganization Management: This is organogram, cage-rattling management that involves fiddling with the structure of the organization. This is the amateur version of process reengineering. Just as people get used to the new structure and system, they are reorganized.

Secrecy Management: This is hush-hush style management. Information is power so it needs to be kept out of the hands of practically everyone. The secret of secrecy management is being "in-the-know" and, more importantly, making sure nobody else is.

Spiritual Management: These are the David Icke type managers who may manifest their style with crystals on their desk or strange pictures on the wall. This is management by shared beliefs; not so much supernatural people as supernatural powers. Believing leads to the release of (mysterious) energy, synergy, ideas, and the like.

Total Obedience Management: This is your no-nonsense, Sergeant-Major, Victorian Gradgrind approach. A manager's job is to give orders, the staff's to obey: Amen. This entire consultative, democratic, first-among-equals stuff is sheer piffle. Manager knows best; tells you what to do; you do it.

Motivating blue-collar workers

The blue/white collar distinction concept appears to have escaped the political correctness police. Thankfully it was not black/white collar, otherwise it would only be the brave, the naive, or the unwise who would still use the term.

The blue/white collar distinction can be variously described with semisynonymous concepts like management/labor; skilled/unskilled; middle class/working class. In essence it describes the nature of the job that people do. White-collar workers are nearly all of managerial grade, while blue-collar workers are those of supervisor and below. "Rude mechanicals" as Shakespeare would have it …

Anyone reading the management literature by academics or gurus may not have noticed that it seems entirely aimed at white-collar workers. Questions about recruitment and selection, motivation and appraisal all seem to apply, almost exclusively, to the relatively well-paid, middle manager types. The work–life balance mantra seems equally applicable only to those privileged enough to have a choice.

The blue/white collar differences are manifest at every level. Ask the two groups about their motives and satisfactions and you may get two completely opposite lists. Skilled, white-collar workers describe their sources of satisfaction in the workplace as: intrinsically interesting work; opportunities to develop skills; the opportunity to see the results of one's labor. Quite low down on the list is good pay. For the unskilled, blue-collar worker, the list of major job satisfactions is in reverse order: good pay, enough help, support and equipment, job security, and so on.

Blue-collar workers have quite different ideas about the nature of the organization from white-collar workers. They differ on what they believe the core values are: indeed, who is part of the organization. They also differ profoundly on what they think the organization is all about.

Blue-collar workers have little truck with all the mission, vision humbug. Their view of the world of work is often refreshingly simple – workers "perform" in exchange for wages. They work hard consistently because there are controls that ensure they do. They are wage slaves; conscripts not volunteers.

The hard question, of course, is how to motivate the blue-collar worker? How do you get the best out of a machine-minder or a product-packer? What to do to get people, gutting chickens all day long in cold, grim factories in a deprived area, to experience job satisfaction?

The stuff of management books seems of little help. How do you enrich a blue-collar job and make it intrinsically satisfying without losing efficiency? How do you get people to identify with an organization they don't fully understand or care less about? Putting them in a uniform does not help much. How do you develop skills where, in essence, you don't need them, the workforce has not got them, or if people really don't want to be developed?

But there is hope. We know that all people at work value involvement, belonging, and feeling valued. The opposite of this experience is alienation with its powerlessness, meaningless, pointlessness.

One motivation technique that has worked for blue-collar workers is the idea of self-managed workteams. That is, rather than have close, oppressive supervision, groups of blue-collar workers "police" themselves. Natural groups of workers are given clear, specific, achievable (if stretchable) targets or goals. *They* then work out how to achieve them. Many certainly get involved because they now have autonomy, albeit limited. They must work out their own rules and methods. They can also very quickly feel a real sense of being valued by their workteam and very loyal to it.

But it is not enough just to set targets, as the present UK government has found. The self-managed workteams need support, particularly at the beginning of the process. They need technical, informational, monetary, and yes, emotional support. They need a few quick wins. They need to feel that they can do it. And when they have, the identification and pride soon flow.

They may even need a bit of (paid) away time to discuss, in their own words and concepts, what it means to be part of a team, the role of leaders, how to handle conflict, and so on. This is not the consultant/guru-led, smart hotel, training program with PowerPoint, *Harvard Business Review*-based graphs. This is about people working it out for themselves.

Interestingly, the process often flushes out some real talent. There is often an "educating Rita" effect, whereby a poorly educated, middle-aged person (often a woman) suddenly shows a real talent for organizing and leading. Others respect them and they suddenly gain tremendous self-respect.

And they need high-profile, public praise for doing a good job. It seems too many companies believe that you motivate the white-collar workers by carrot and the blue workers by stick. The guys at the top respond to big bonuses; guys at the bottom to threats of layoffs.

Self-management is about that dreaded late eighties word *empowerment*. For some this meant taking on supervisory responsibility but with no concomitant reward. In some organizations it was enthusiastically resisted by managers who feared losing power, authority, even their jobs, and for staff who felt neither able nor recognized for the additional burden. But it was also found to be immensely important and successful in certain jobs which had previously been considered impossible to be made motivating except by small carrot and big stick.

Self-managed work groups give blue-collar workers a sense of autonomy, involvement, and belonging. It takes time, effort, and money to set them up, and continual support thereafter. But they remain probably the best way to make otherwise tedious and alienating jobs bearable.

The N-word

We have known for twenty years the three best predictors of success at work. But if you read popular books about, or attend advanced courses on, recruitment and selection you would never guess what they are. And, paradoxically, they are almost never measured or fully enquired into at interviews or even at assessment centres.

They are intelligence (cognitive ability/capacity), emotional stability, and conscientiousness (the work ethic). The opposite of stability is neuroticism and it should be a strong select-out factor at work.

So what is neuroticism? Why are some people neurotic and others not? What does it mean to be neurotic ? Can neuroses be cured? But most importantly – why is neuroticism a (serious) problem in (most) workplaces?

The etymology of neurosis is nerves. It is dictionary-defined as "a nervous disorder (unaccompanied by disease of the nervous system) in which one or more phobias, compulsions or obsessions is accompanied, usually by anxiety, making normal life difficult".

Perhaps the first serious personality theorist, Galen, the Greek philosopher, recognized the central role of neuroticism in his four humors. Extraverted neurotics (the choleric) are touchy, restless, aggressive, excitable, and changeable, while introverted neurotics (the melancholic) are moody, anxious, rigid, sober, and pessimistic.

Around 120 years ago an American psychiatrist called Beard used the word neurasthenia, which means "weakness of the nerves". The symptoms were lack of energy and physical complaints. Fifty years ago the American Psychiatric Association defined psychoneurotic disorder thus:

> The chief characteristic of these disorders is "anxiety" which may be directly felt and expressed, or which may be unconsciously and automatically controlled by the utilization of various psychological defense mechanisms (depression, conversion, displacement). Longitudinal (lifelong) studies of individuals with such disorders usually present evidence of periodic or constant maladjustment of varying degree from early life. Special stress may bring about acute symptomatic expression of such disorders.

In fact psychiatrists have in recent times dropped the term neurosis because they have split it up into more specific orders such as mood, anxiety, and somatoform disorders. And the politically-correct-police don't like the term either, insisting on *negative affectivity*.

But personality theorists and psychometric test developers have no gripe about using the term. One famous psychologist said simply that neurosis is a term used to describe maladaptive behavior associated with strong emotions. Paradoxically, neurotics know their behavior is nonsensical, absurd, or irrelevant, but feel powerless to change it. Further, modern researchers have shown it to be biologically based and substantially heritable.

There is wide agreement that neurosis can take many forms: phobias, compulsions, proneness to depression, hypochondriasis. But all neurotics share a general tendency to experience strong emotional reactions, such as anger, disgust, embarrassment, fear, guilt, and sadness. They are moody (unstable) and their powerful, disruptive emotions interfere with their day-to-day adaptation. This means they can be prone to odd ideas and have poor strategies for coping with stress.

Some neurotics are apprehensive, fearful, prone to worry, jittery, tense, and nervous. They are of course prone to phobias and anxiety-based illnesses like headaches and ulcers. Others manifest their instability through anger and hostility. They tend to be bitter, resentful, and easily frustrated.

A more common facet of neurosis is associated with depression. They are, at work, easily discouraged and dejected. Their emotions are dominated by guilt, hopelessness, loneliness, and sadness.

Neurotics tend to be self-consciousness. They can seem shy and uncomfortable around others. They are certainly easily embarrassed, sensitive to shame and ridicule. They can have feelings of inferiority which lead to withdrawal. They are certainly vulnerable to work stress. They can easily feel dependent or panicked when faced with difficult work situations. They appear helpless, hapless, and hopeless with difficult situations.

Identifying neurotics has important implications for how they behave at work. It tells one about coping with everyday stresses. By and large, neurotics have poor coping strategies – they are less rational and more emotional than they should be. They can be hostile, or prone to self-blame, even to escapist fantasies. Interestingly, they know their strategies are not good but they seem powerless to change or improve them.

Neurotics are often oversensitive to monitoring their health and responding to physical problems and illnesses. This of course leads to high absenteeism. Psychologists note that it may be particularly important to seek objective confirmation of reported symptoms where possible. Neuroticism is of course also closely linked to happiness and general well-being. Neurotics see the glass half-empty. They seem more sensitive to life's problems than its rewards and seek support more than they give it. They need support and sympathy. They are moody and volatile and rather unpredictable.

While it is true that extraverts excel in certain jobs and introverts in others, it is not at all clear where neuroticism is an advantage. A touch of obsessiveness may help in certain jobs that involve checking and monitoring, but neuroticism is related to absenteeism and accidents at work; gloom and doom; negativity and low morale; therapy and counseling; job dissatisfaction and low productivity.

That is why study after study shows a very robust finding. Stable, stress-resistant, even-tempered, robust, and resilient individuals do well at work. They are the opposite of neurotics. They are dependable, hardy, and cheerful. It's not much fun having a neurotic boss, co-worker, or subordinate.

The narcissism business

Vanity is a great motivator. In the UK, the honors system of patronage may have innumerable detractors, but it certainly motivates a good deal of charity work, not to mention party donations.

But the commercial world has not been slow in exploiting this most deep-seated and darkest of need. One growing manifestation is the Who's Who business.

The red original *Who's Who* is a flourishing British institution that started in 1849. It is subtitled *An Annual Biographical Dictionary* and contains over 30,000 entries. Everyone "in the know" is clear about the signs of having made it in life: a decent gong, a *Who's Who* entry, or an invitation to appear on Desert Island Discs. Of course a hat trick of obits in the broadsheets is much desired, but one is unlikely to appreciate it fully!

Who's Who is *the* list of the eminent. How you are chosen is a mystery, strangely comforting to those who have crossed the barrier and remain in "for life". And deeply frustrating for those who don't know why they have not been selected. Periodically there are witch hunts; investigative journalism attempts to find out how the system works.

The result: the ins and not ins; the quietly smug and the outrageously discriminated against. It is a deep wound against pride, even vanity, perhaps narcissism.

And seeing a need, in tiptoe the entrepreneurs. Why should there be only one *Who's Who*? Don't like the system? Start your own. There is surely a large army of people eager to sign up for inclusion and buy – at outrageous prices – thick books of thousand upon thousand, never-made-its hungry for recognition.

The Americans – that nation of self-esteem enthusiasts – got into the game first. Now, the old Imperial power who invents everything but has to be taught how to exploit those inventions is catching up fast.

Who's Who has proliferated to meet the apparently insatiable demand to have one's achievements acknowledged. People in the headlines, and many who are not, will attest to being bombarded by offers to appear in yet another of these weighty tomes.

They come in essentially three forms. There is the Who's Who in Nowhereville approach. This is done by geographic region. And of course driven by demand. Areas are getting smaller. Soon you may come across Who's Who in Iowa, or the Mid-Oklahoma Who's Who.

A second type is Who's Who by "achievement area". So we can have Who's Who in science or medicine, engineering, or manufacturing. Of course Joe Blow who runs the local drugstore may feel he deserves mention in them all. But if he and others like him want to appear just wait for Who's Who in retail pharmaceuticals.

The third type is the brashly alternative book that eschews the words Who's Who and goes for titles like "International Biographies of Achievement" or some such.

The clues to the nature of the enterprise and the narcissism that it feeds are twofold. First, just when the letter of congratulations on the wonderful achievements and a lifetime of service arrives, so does an order form for the book. Two things are noticeable. The cost is often very high, starting at $200 plus. And, given that people may be squashed 20 to the page, that's a lot for a moment of glory. Next, the book always comes in various forms: no frills but nevertheless very expensive, leather-bound, gold embossed, and so on. This means the book is a record, a trophy, a treasure for all time. So why not cough up the extra for a pig-skinned, fine old craftsman, parchment paper edition?

The second, even more obvious giveaway, is the "mention a friend" section. This is usually dressed up as "assist our researchers" but means in effect "Do you know some gullible, vain person like yourself?" The problem with this of course is that it reduces exclusivity. Half the thrill of being in a Who's Who is knowing that your friends are not.

All this may be a sign of that most common and dangerous of personality disorders: narcissism. It is a potential derailer but, paradoxically, narcissism can serve business people very well.

So what are the markers of narcissism? The narcissistic manager is marked by grandiosity (in fantasy or behavior), need for admiration, and lack of empathy. Self-centred, selfish, egotistical: narcissists are everywhere in business – alas.

1. They have a grandiose sense of self-importance (for example exaggerated achievements and talents, expectation to be recognized as superior without commensurate achievements).
2. Most are preoccupied with fantasies of unlimited success, power, brilliance, and money.
3. They believe that they are "special" and unique and can only be understood by, or should associate with, other special or high-status people (or institutions). They may try to "buy" themselves into exclusive circles.

4. They require excessive admiration and respect from everyone at work, always.
5. Bizarrely, often they have a sense of entitlement, that is, unreasonable expectations of favorable treatment or automatic compliance with their manifest needs.
6. Worse, they take advantage of others to achieve their own ends, which makes them terrible managers.
7. They lack empathy. All are unwilling to recognize or identify with the feelings and needs of others. They have desperately low EQ.
8. Curiously, they are often envious of others and believe that others are envious of them.
9. They show arrogant, haughty behaviors or attitudes all the time and everywhere at work (and home). At times this can be pretty amusing, but is mostly simply frustrating.

Narcissism is full-blown vanity. Narcissists want to buy *Who's Who* rather than merely appear in it. But the journey from ambition to narcissism may not be that long. And the line between arrogance, vanity, and narcissism is a thin one.

Beware the bright, good-looking, ambitious narcissists. They are very dangerous. For them all business is the narcissism business.

Pep up your creativity

People in the public sector are not thought of as creative. But most people like to think they are – or at least could be. Hence the popularity of courses and programs.

Some "creatives" rejoice in the term and help you to identify them by giving clues to their chosen and much celebrated status. The men wear bow ties, ponytails, white suits. They may have ultramodern spectacles, carry tripods or wear idiosyncratic clothes or jewellery. The more desperate change their name from Chuck to Zin Zan, buy Botox treatment and try highly unorthodox diets. They are, quite rightly, insecure about their creative juices. Real creatives are, however, as we can see from biographies, somewhat different.

Creativity, like every other human characteristic from head size to foot size, from intelligence to integrity, and from mathematical to musical ability, is normally distributed. Most of us are a little above or below average although we all very happily endorse the Lake Wobegon effect where all the women are strong, all the men are good-looking, and all the children are above average.

We are, it seems, most unhappy to accept the possibility that we may be below average. However, with such things as height or hairiness, weight or width, it may be relatively difficult to deny.

Thanks to self-help books, snake-oil salesmen, naiveté, and desperation, people believe that whatever they were dished out in the lottery of life is capable of *great improvement*. "Everyone is (or can be) creative", explain trainers and consultants who dwell in that refreshingly evidence-free zone of life.

Alas, everyone can't be tall – even with surgery or subtle shoe wear. Nor can everyone be slim. We seem to take the former, if not the latter, for granted.

But, given our "base level" of creativity can we raise our game? Although not well understood, or researched for that matter, it seems that creativity is a function of intelligence, personality, thinking style, motivation, and an environment that genuinely encourages it. It seems we can learn to be more creative by using a few tricks of the trade.

It is these "tricks" which are taught on expensive creativity programs that seem a mixture between an elementary school classroom with the teacher on speed and a revivalist meeting with an old-style preacher.

Here are some simple but important ideas:

Sleep on it: Come back to problems and issues. Let them lie fallow for a bit; stew; incubate. Revisit them when it suits.

Read widely: Talk to all sorts of experts. Get outside your box. Talk to people who think about things differently from you.

Don't give up: Persistence is the key. Most attempts fail. Breakthroughs are rare.

Take a risk: Fear of failure, humiliation, teasing, and abuse are natural enemies of creativity. Go on – play with hunches and tentative ideas. Break the rules. Take courage.

Piggyback: Take others' work and take it further. Put things together which do not fit.

Identify peak times and conditions: Work out when and where you are at your best for idea generation and refinement. Set aside these times for those activities.

Record your flashes: Have a place and method to record all ideas – some worth revisiting and incubation.

Build your particular expertise/skill/knowledge: creativity is always skill based. Get to the cutting edge of your chosen area – there is no substitute for this.

Question and probe the obvious: Take little for granted; turn things upside down; celebrate similarities and differences.

Lighten up: Be playful; use humor; have a sense of the absurd and the ridiculous.

Rocket science? No. Counterintuitive? Perhaps. But these are "tricks of the trade". They are well known to those really interested in novelty and solving problems. They are also the ideas dressed up with jargon and fun-and-games in creativity workshops. And, by the way, wearing a bow tie and being called Raphael or Donatello won't help one at all.

Performance appraisal systems

Performance appraisal systems: pointless paper chase or powerful motivational tool? Most people in the public sector, and many in the private, are deeply skeptical and cynical about performance appraisal. They have seen HR departments chop and change "the form" endlessly, been on various workshops, filled in staff surveys – and still receive perfunctory appraisals and an apology for performance-related pay.

Performance management systems (PMS) are a powerful tool of change. They were used in the 1980s and 90s to try to change the whole public sector culture and ethos. There are profound value differences between the old *service culture* and the new *performance culture*.

The service culture was based on the principle of experience and equality. People in the same job with the same experience (and qualifications) expected and got the same pay and had roughly the same prospects of promotion. In the process of "doing one's time," one gained experience, showed loyalty and commitment, and learned the corporate culture. You waited your turn.

In the UK, people were paid equally for equal work – or at least being in the same job. The unions liked that and bargained and negotiated for pay for specific levels. Annual appraisals were not taken seriously and often not conducted at all – there was not much point.

And then a new ethic appeared. This was based on equity, not equality, and the new word was "performance". You are rewarded for what you do and you need help and clear feedback on a regular basis from your boss on how you are doing. You need specific goals and targets with measurable success criteria (KRAs, KPIs), regular progress reviews, and a meaningful annual appraisal. Data have to be collected on performance and these serve as the basis for all decision making. Radical stuff.

It has been known for 80 years that (by and large) the best worker produced about two-and-a-half times as much as the least productive worker. The equity principle says that input should relate equitably to output and therefore every worker's "reward package" should be directly related to his/her productivity.

Therefore, and here's the tough bit, two people in the same job and with the same experience should not be paid the same unless their pro-

ductivity is the same. Equal pay was only fair if there was equal output –
and patently there was not. And, equally important, it meant really *measuring output*. You cannot manage what you do not measure – as the new
mantra went.

Many people in the public sector were aghast. Their currency was now
useless. It did not matter how long they had served: it was all about their
productivity which was now subject to measurement. Not only were years
of service deemed irrelevant (and sometimes even pitiable), but these
people now felt under surveillance.

Once the new system was explained, the most common reaction (after
shock, horror, and anger) was to explain that it seemed a good idea *but for
others*. "You see," the old-fashioned public sector employee explained
(patronizingly) "*our* output cannot be measured". How do you measure
the output of a nurse, or a social worker, or a policeman, or a university
teacher? … impossible … and therefore (alas) we cannot use the system.
So the PMS supporters enquired how organizations made decisions about
promotion, training, and so on – was it based only on time-serving? "No,
of course not!", came the defence "it is based on performance". But how
is that measured/assessed? Silence.

In the brave days of the 1980s when Thatcherism was an unstoppable
force, many public bodies in the UK were cajoled into reworking their
PMS and many experimented with an equitable pay-for-performance
system. Needless to say it was strongly resisted at various levels. It is not
difficult to sabotage these systems and this was done.

The problem lay not so much in measuring performance, although that
is not easy, but in inequitable reward. What does an organization do if it
shows the best do two-and-a-half times as much as the worst? Pay them
two-and-a-half times as much, perhaps?

Chaos, disenchantment, and resistance led to revision of the system.
The measurement was kept, and the appraisals had to be done and the
(damn) forms filled out. But the performance-related-reward bit was
fudged. The difference between the top award and the bottom was very
small (often a couple of hundred pounds). So the principle of equity was
creeping back to the old principle of equality.

But now no one was happy. All the bureaucracy remained: you have
to be trained to conduct appraisals, you have to prove you have done them,
you have to fill out the form – but it seems to have few consequences. Further, the worst employees remain jealous and the best demotivated
because the promise was not kept.

For many this is where we are today. This is the "third way" of performance appraisal.

The key ingredient of performance appraisal is common sense. It means *agreeing* targets or objectives so that managers get the best out of their staff. Next it means *supporting* them fully in their attempt to hit these targets. And it means giving them helpful *feedback* on how they are doing not only on a daily, highly specific level, but also on a more general level. This feedback should consider the big picture, the long term, and the developmental opportunities for the individual. And this feedback is called "performance appraisal".

So what to do? All employees need some idea of what their manager wants from them (goals), they need feedback on how they are doing (appraisals), and they need to be rewarded for their effort. That is common sense. The hard bit is the reward and whether it is equitable.

Personal development

Investment in people; development plans; executive training: a waste of time and money or an essential activity? Discuss.

Fans of personal development argue there is clear, unambiguous, and "scientific" evidence for return on investment. Companies spend fortunes on management and sales training. They sponsor MBAs at often $30–50k/£20–30k per head. Some people are "sheep dipped" on mass programs. Others are more individually coached, taught, or apprenticed.

Naturally companies want reassurance, preferably empirical evidence, that all this outlay actually works. Many are happy to reduce their dissonance, guilt, or shareholder skepticism by linking some sales, revenue, market-share growth figures with some developmental intervention. Is training in essence an expense or an investment?

But it doesn't take a rocket scientist to point out that it is seriously difficult to really measure any impact of people development. Many variables affect business success and it is difficult to isolate one while controlling others. Individual and organization performance fluctuates – so when to measure results? Directly after training and workshops, or six months down the line? Should one seek hard evidence expressed in time, money, or some other behavioral measure, or be happy with staff and customer feedback on change? Is it better to have those business-school type measures like marginal utility of the program, years to break even, or statistical effect sizes? Is it possible to measure the costs of not investing in people? What kinds of organizations do and don't get involved in all this malarkey?

It is possible to plot money spent on training/development against stock market performance over a set period. And depending on whose side you are on it is not difficult to find evidence for your prejudices. Some graphs and figures reassure the investor and one can confidently conclude that when development is planned, structured, and aligned with business strategy (blah, blah), it leads to profit, a culture based on employee commitment and customer focus, increased managerial proficiency, and so on.

Some companies swear by it to aid recovery after declining market share, unhappy restructuring, or a messy M&A. But others like the corporate culture talk of continuous improvement, constant feedback, and so on.

Other organizations believe all those negative signs of absenteeism, turnover, poor morale, weak leadership, poor planning, internal conflict, short-term focus, loss of talent, and so on, are the result of no or poor development. The enthusiasts believe talent has to be nurtured and developed – not just found and selected for. People have to be grown so that their competence, commitment, readiness, and satisfaction are just right.

As has been said, "there is no alternative". Cynics and skeptics seem less convinced. And the more they have been trained in scientific thinking, the more they are unimpressed by the evidence. Correlation is not cause. Multiple factors are in play.

The way to really check the issue is take a big department of, say, salespeople in the same company with similar experience, talent, and potential. Put a third through a preferred program; let a third just get on with it; make a third do fitness training. Measure their performance before, immediately after, and some time later. That is better evidence. Too difficult to do for most people, alas.

Even the enthusiasts admit more than one way of doing development. Off the job (expensive business school, hotel) may not always be the best solution. There are now many alternatives, some much cheaper than others: web-based development, mentoring, coaching, work shadowing, job rotation, project/team-based learning ... each different in style, philosophy, and perhaps outcome.

Cautious skeptics are difficult to persuade that many programs really work in the sense that they really influence the bottom line. All those leadership programs about self-awareness, understanding complexity, leading change, motivating the demotivated, new ways of seeing, and so on, seem to promise more than they offer. Most know others who have been on them and appear to have received little or no benefit whatsoever.

Few disagree that companies need to attract leverage and motivator talent specialists. They also believe it is important to retain and enlarge the best. The question is how. And the current state of the data means the jury is still out.

The personality of interviewers

Even the most structured competency-based interviews are aimed at collecting data about the personality of interviewees. There are countless books for interviewing professionals on what traits to look for, what questions to ask, and how to interpret the answers to those tricky, perspicacious questions. But there is no explicit recognition that the personality of the *interviewer* may play a very significant role in the whole interview process. So do *different* types/personalities make *different* decisions on the *same* people given the *same* criteria? Presumably they know what they are looking for and have agreed specific criteria in terms of a candidate's abilities, attitudes, experiences, personality, and values. So why is there ever any disagreement? Were the criteria not clear? Did the questions not elicit data to satisfy the criteria? Often both of these are true. But there remains one other factor – differences in the personalities of the interviewers which have to be factored into this equation.

Extraverts usually enjoy interviewing. They are "people people" – sociable, eager to be amused and entertained, and entertaining. Extraverts probably talk too much and listen too little. They may not do their preparation as thoroughly as they should. They may be impatient and inattentive in long interviews. And of course they are attracted to vivacious (if vacuous) candidates.

Introverts make very different, and often diffident, interviewers. They pause more, seeming hesitant, when they are processing information. They can find the whole process tiring and intimidating, and feel more for those candidates who are similar to themselves. They usually take the data gathering more seriously and see the whole interview less as a social occasion than a semi-scientific exercise. Certainly the introverted candidate probably gets a "better deal" (a more favorable hearing) from the introverted interviewer. The trouble is that introverts eschew, while extraverts volunteer for interviewing assignments.

And what of the "sensitive" (neurotic) interviewer? They are the fragile flowers of the world, often hypersensitive to real and imaginary threats. They are stress-prone and don't like people in general, whom they see as threatening. They can be bitchy and critical, wary and judgmental.

Neurotic interviewers can easily feel threatened by the potential "mover and shaker". They worry about things: the future, the present; their reputation, their security; their ability, their respect-worthiness, and so on. They listen carefully to the candidates' answers to questions about work–life balance, diversity, counseling, and other issues. If they don't like what they hear in response to salient as well as less relevant questions, their instinct is to push the rejection button.

Stable interviewers, like stable employees, are better news. They are less irritable and moody, and better able to weigh the information. They worry less about what might go wrong and cope with all the little dramas at interviews well. They tend to be calm, focused, and rational.

What of the personality trait "agreeableness"? Agreeable interviewers are warm, empathic, and trusting. They are for the most part likeable. They understand that interviews can be stressful. They are concerned about making candidates comfortable, relaxed, and able to be their real selves. They are slow to chide and swift to bless, and believe they get the best out of others by giving them a chance.

Less agreeable and likeable interviewers believe you understand people best by "putting them on the spot". They treat the interview as a political interview. They cross-examine individuals, often pushing them to give details of success and failure which their résumé overlooks. They are hard to please: cynical, tough, world-weary, and they care little for interviewee comfort.

Conscientious interviewers are not only conscientious about how they approach the task of interviewing, but also what they are looking for. Hard work is a virtue. Some are even prepared to "trade off" ability for the work ethic: preferring the loyal plodder to the capricious wunderkind. Conscientious interviewers are concerned that the applicant follows orders, obeys rules, and has a sense of duty.

Less conscientious interviewers want to have fun. They tend to be less achievement oriented, less careful, and with a much weaker work ethic. All that "postponement of gratification" stuff never worked with them. They prefer what the Freudians call "the pleasure principle". They seek out playmates more than solid and reliable colleagues.

The ambition and achievement needs of interviewers are also relevant. Paradoxically, both the low and the high ambition interviewer may be intimidated by the obviously ambitious candidate. Those with low ambitions can feel intimidated by newly minted MBAs who want to be on the board at 30 and retired at 40. The highly ambitious see a potential threat.

What of the abilities of the interviewer? How are bright, educated interviewers different from their less talented peers? Another paradox: the clever prefer discriminating questions, the dim prefer "clever" questions. Brighter people tend to have a bigger vocabulary and think fast. They ask good questions which sort the wheat from the chaff.

The less bright and less educated interviewers might rehearse "killer" questions that make them appear intelligent, even if they cannot process the answers. They can be intimidated in group interviews and behave badly. They often have "crackpot" theories, refreshingly evidence free about desirable characteristics in candidates.

The interview is a social process. It can be a sophisticated intellectual, theatrical show; a hall of mirrors; a game of bluff and counterbluff. There is no doubt that there is a lot of "gut feeling" going on in both parties, despite all their training.

So the moral of the story? First, acknowledge that the interviewers' makeup (ability and personality) does inevitably play a part. Second, try to work out how specific interviewers react to particular candidates. Third, use multiple interviewers but particularly those with the ability and personality profiles found among those actually doing the job in question. Fourth, where possible, encourage these insights in interviewers. Fifth, choose (yes, and train) interviewers who are bright, stable, and conscientious.

Pouring money down the drain

The outcome of the UK's next election may well be determined by debates about the efficiency of the public sector, especially in education and health. Labour's traditional *tax and spend* policies appear to have failed yet again. Despite dramatic increases in public spending there appears to be no corresponding increase in output and efficiency. Why?

The first reason relates to the simple idea that there is a clear correspondence between *pay and performance*. This is not, nor has it ever been, true. Perceived low pay can and does lead to considerable dissatisfaction and demotivation but not vice versa.

The effects of a pay rise very soon wear off as people *adapt* to their new conditions. Any improvements are therefore likely to be very temporary.

Second, what leads to pay satisfaction is not so much absolute salary but *comparative* salary. So if my salary goes up dramatically, but so does that of my comparison group, there is no change in my behavior.

Third, money is *not everything*. Many would be happy with more time off or more job security rather than more money. Finally, there is the eternal implication of tax and spend ... all very well to increase pay, but if increased *taxes* eat heavily into it where is the benefit?

Many people in health and education saw salary increases merely as government attempts to "catch up" with the times: to align pay and conditions with the private sector. It was, and is, an attempt at the restitution of justice.

Another big error is to assume a simple, linear and *causal* relationship between spending and efficiency that goes something like this: make people happy at work (with nice offices, free meals, and so on) and they experience work satisfaction. This in turn leads to greater performance and efficiency.

But there is very little good evidence that satisfaction *leads* to productivity. It is the same mistake made about self-esteem, where it is assumed that esteem leads to achievement, happiness, and success *rather than the other way around*.

It may be much wiser to invest in better productivity than in satisfaction, because the causal path is more that way round. Thus the productive worker is better rewarded, more positively appraised, and gains more confidence.

The public sector still reflects the *service* rather than the *performance* ethic. Loyalty, years of service, and a clean-sheet reputation determine promotion much more than performance measured by output, customer feedback, and so on.

If you want efficiency you have to measure it, understand the process, set goals/targets, and reward their achievement. You need to understand how teams work together in doing so. It is easy to set goals: harder to measure and understand *how* they are achieved. If there is no clear relationship between effort and reward by individuals and their team, there seems little incentive to be more productive.

An entrepreneur would soon stop pouring money down the drain if he or she thought that spending was not leading to efficiency. They would first start looking at delivery systems and structures to see if they were working properly. If not there would be a strong dose of *process reengineering*. Yes, that fad is a bit passé now, but the idea is fundamental.

Is efficiency a function of a poorly designed system that can be improved? If yes, redesign – even if there is a lot of resistance.

If the systems and structure are OK, select and *train* people to work them well. This may mean losing those unable or unwilling to adopt new ways of working. The motto is *"be happy here or be happy elsewhere"*. Then make sure you have a way to identify and reward productivity and efficiency equitably.

No quick fix alas … hard words for politicians to hear. But otherwise so little effect for so much tax payers' money. And when they understand that, it seems quite reasonable to turn to others who may have some better ideas, a longer view, and more courage to make changes that really work.

Projective techniques

Ever wondered why psychologists use inkblots? Would chicken entrails do as well? Or the tea leaves so rarely seen in our tea-bagged society? What's the theory?

The Swiss psychologist Rorschach invented the inkblot technique. It still has a small and evidence-defying cult following. The idea is simple, the interpretation unreliable and complex. The inkblot is called in the jargon "a projective technique". The idea is that one projects onto the inkblot shapes one's motives, needs, fears, and the like, which one cannot articulate to oneself or others. Supposedly the skilled and trained researcher can do the correct reading.

Most of us have probably during adolescence been exposed to a party game projective technique. You are on a walk, and going through a forest. You come across a stream/river. Please describe it. Next to the river is a hut. Again describe it. Ahead of you is a road through the forest. What is it like?

The budding psychologist does the interpretation. Whatever you say (the river is deep, the river is shallow, the river has rocks) is deeply symbolic of our frustrated unconscious needs for sex, power, or domination. A simple game apparently says more about you than you know yourself. It is not only your cleverly hidden secrets, but things you don't know about yourself that appear to emerge from projective technique analysis.

The idea behind this technique is that people *cannot* rather than *will not* tell you their real needs, drives, and fears. This is not a matter of will or ability.

We don't have sufficient insight into our real needs. Most of us know of individuals who genuinely believe they have a sense of humor. Everyone around them knows they don't. Whence the difference? Others can think they are caring and empathic when the evidence is that they are egocentric and disagreeable.

There are two other more recent and scientifically more respectable projective techniques. The first dates back to before World War II and is called the thematic apperception test (TAT). It consists of 20 or so pictures. You are shown them one at a time and your job is to tell a short story associated with each. These are transcribed and coded for themes about need for affiliation, need for power, need for achievement, and so on.

The first picture is a little boy looking at a violin. But what is your story? An unhappy little boy forced to go to violin lessons by a tyrannical mother when he would rather be playing conkers? A sad little deaf boy knowing he will never hear the sweet music of the violin? A triumphant little boy who has mastered a tune before his peers?

Then the next picture, and so on. All are obviously from another era. None is racy, but number 13 is most interesting. A woman (possibly naked) lies on a bed/sofa shrouded by a see-through curtain; a fully dressed man peers out of the window. What is your version of events?

There is one other technique which has also done the rounds. It's called sentence completion. Strictly speaking it is only a partial projective technique because it is more transparent than either the Rorschach or the TAT. You are given, say, 20 sentences to complete. They may be simple like: "Most people's suffering is due to ... ", to more complex short stories that require completion.

Critics of projective techniques say they are deeply unreliable in two senses of the word. First, a person's mood seems to affect their responses, so they give rather different answers at different times. This cannot then give us a veridical picture of their profound, stable, deep-seated needs. Second, and more important, scoring is unreliable. Even two experts don't seem to agree on the "real meaning" of the output.

Scientists say that what is unreliable cannot be valued. Amen. And so projective techniques inhabit a twilight world between cult and science, between old and new techniques, between the past and future of psychometrics.

But despite all this, one fact remains patently true. Getting at a person's motivations is difficult. Every manager wants to know what motivates their staff. They want to know the magic buttons. Most recognize there are wide individual differences. And the clever ones know that money and titles are but part of the story.

Motivation is about force and direction. Just as there are fundamental differences in libido – motivation or appetite for sex – so there are at work. Some people are driven. They always have been; they always will be. Maybe they are driven by being rather short or uneducated; maybe they are driven by a clearly preferred and successful sibling; maybe they are driven to fulfil long-suppressed and forgotten parental expectations.

The light can be bright or dim. Some people are more hungry than others. But for what and why? What drives people to try to make more and more money; more than they could ever spend; what drives them to repeat disastrous relationships again and again; why are people so obsessed by trivial things like job titles?

It is certainly true that many people cannot tell you. They can offer descriptions and explanations, and may even be practiced in the art, but they ring hollow to the informed outsider.

A good counselor, coach, or psychologist might help. Those with insightful, psychological mindedness can assist. Some seek insight; others avoid it. It is said that many comics shun analysts lest they take away that drive, their edge, their special power. Their very "raison d'être" is destroyed by self-insight into why they think and act as they do.

All very interesting, but how does this help the selector in the day-to-day business of trying to choose managers who are able and driven to achieve? Not much, alas. But it does quite strongly warn to dig a little deeper, to look for patterns, and not to be satisfied with glib answers.

Protecting your legacy

Powerful people of a certain age and stage often ponder their legacy. What will they leave behind? How will history remember them? And, indeed, what can they do now to ensure a favorable mark in posterity?

Do senior people sometimes take their eye off the ball as a result of being too concerned with their legacy and so, paradoxically and ironically, destroy it?

People do very strange things to try to influence history. Some try to destroy all their papers so no record is left. Others selectively remove, edit, and insert forged documents to try to confuse historians of the future. Some spend lavishly to buy forgiveness in their later years for what passed in earlier times. Others search for biographers "deeply sympathetic" to their side of the story.

Those who, like all of us, seek to "live on" but have the means to do so usually try various methods.

The first is *philanthropical*: donate money to a cause. Educational institutions always seem worthy recipients. The very successful business-man Lord Wolfson had colleges named after him at both Oxford and Cam-bridge, being the only person apart from Jesus Christ to have this honor. Sometimes you simply give away money at the rate and speed that you made it – hoping that the parable about the camel, the eye of the needle and heaven will then not apply.

Even if not wealthy, a charitable foundation can be started. Here one thinks of the UK's Cheshire Homes where a famous fighter ace dedicated his long life to saving rather than killing people. But this is usually a life-long quest, not simply a preretirement activity.

Another possible legacy is something *physical*: perhaps the pyramids are the most dramatic example. The idea is to have a physical monument: a great library (think of recent American presidents) bearing one's name; a folly perhaps; a grand house. Hadrian is remembered for his wall – and little else.

A third method is *legal*: this is an attempt to introduce an eponymous law that will create more justice. Wilberforce is remembered for stopping slavery. But this method is very difficult unless you are a politician.

Another method is to *write*: plays, books, poems, or indeed the modern equivalent of producing films or TV programs. The trouble with this method is that it takes both time and talent.

What happens to CEOs when their thoughts turn to their real or likely or desirable legacy? What is it they want history to say of them: they were just and kind? They turned things around? They had both courage and wisdom?

Occasionally on training courses for serious grown-ups the instructors ask people to write their own obituary. This is not meant to examine writing ability or indeed to prove one can still remember what one has done. The real reason is to look back and note real achievements; those that others recognize and will last. In this task scribblers often lurch between hubris and humility, both of which are inappropriate. The lesson is to sort the wheat from the chaff: to distinguish the transient from the long lasting, the real achievements vs the trivial.

It is said that Nobel (he of the prizes) having read his own obituary, which was of course an error, decided to give all his money away. He did not want to be remembered for having made a fortune from explosives. Rather he wanted his name associated with great discoveries in science, great literature, and peace, not war.

There is a real danger that these legacy dreams and plans influence the present. A CEO is responsible to many shareholders. It is the CEO's job to ensure the business is viable, productive, and profitable. And that it weathers the storm of globalization and the turbulence of the stock market. The best strategy is to concentrate on that with energy and passion. That in itself is legacy enough.

The psychology of color

Virgin has a bright saturated red; Barclays a distinctive turquoise; Lufthansa a goldy-yellow and BP a range of greeny yellows. Aer Lingus's green has changed over the years as did Air Canada's red.

In our culture there are color codes. Red is the danger color: it means halt, stop, prohibited, on fire. Yellow and black used together mean warning; danger. Black lettering on a yellow background is the optimum for legibility. Green means safety, exit, rescue services. Blue is for helpful signage.

Color can be used to enhance various perceptual effects like distance, temperature, and excitement. Red, yellow, violet, and brown "bring things closer", while blue and green help make things look further away. Orange and yellow imply warmth; blue and green are cool colors. And green (mental hospital green in particular) is meant to be "restful", while red is stimulating and violet aggressive. Supposedly so, but what is the quality of the evidence?

Designers and marketing people take color seriously. Color has symbolic value. Color creates impressions. Color can be memorable. But does it influence behavior over the long term? Can you make people happier and more productive at work through subtle use of color?

You may be able to make a (deceptively small) room look bigger through colored paint or light. Or you may make a cold room look and "feel" cosy. But do people behave differently for any length of time with these different perceptions?

A lot of nonsense is spoken about color. This is the evidence-free, naively enthusiastic world of color therapy, color consultants, and color designers. There is an army of barmy chromophiles offering psychological diagnoses and interventions. One can change or enhance image by colors: you can become more intellectual if you wear blue-grays or blue-greens or muted blues; appear more secure if you combine earth tones or deep shades of colors with "bright accents" of gold, ivory, or white.

The first question is, do consistent color preferences exist? And are these preferences related to the characteristics of individuals? The answer is yes – but the research is patchy. Females show greater preference for red, violet, and yellow, and more dislike of green than males. They also prefer highly saturated, brighter colors than males. But we don't know if this is true in other cultures and historical periods, or indeed why this sex difference occurs. There is evidence that color preference is culturally learned, as different colors have very different associations in different cultures. This inevitably limits the generalization of these findings.

Extraverts tend to prefer arousing, warm colors (red) while introverts prefer calming, cool colors (green). Extraverts choose and prefer bright, pure colors, whereas introverts prefer more subtle shades. Sensation seekers prefer red, low sensation seekers prefer blue.

Young children seem to associate different colors with different emotions: love, anger, pain with red and black; happiness, strength, "life" with blue; honesty with white. As they get older children shift away from a preference for warmer colors (especially yellow) to cooler colors (especially blue).

Dark-eyed people tend to prefer colors at the red end of the spectrum, light-eyed people at the blue end. This is probably due to the presence of a pigment, melanin, in dark-eyed people which acts as a light shield.

It is true that colors have symbolic associations. Red – charity, divine love. Green – faith, gladness, hope, and joy. Black – wisdom, constancy, as well as evil, falsehood, error. White – purity, truth. Blue – hope, faith, modesty, and fidelity. Yellow – jealousy and change.

There are idioms and adages which refer to color. We talk about being "off color", "coming out with flying colors", "sailing under false colors". There is also "feeling blue" and "green with envy".

Certainly colors in the environment are known to affect mood. In general, colors at the long wavelength end of the spectrum such as red and orange, can induce feelings of high arousal, while short wavelength colors, such as blue and green, induce feelings of calm.

A number of studies have made comparisons of the arousal properties of various pairs of colors. Thus, violet has been shown to produce greater arousal than green; red produces more arousal than blue. Red lighting produces greater arousal than either blue or green.

The above demonstrations used measures of physiological arousal. At a more subjective level, it has also been found that people feel more excited and stimulated by red, orange, and yellow than by green and blue. Blue tends to associate more with feelings of being calm, peaceful, and serene. Green has no strong association at a psychological level with such descriptions of how one feels.

There are various ways in which color can affect how well people learn new things or perform on educational tasks. Color coding has helped people distinguish between broad categories of things and actions (for example hot/cold, on/off). Coding has helped people develop maps of their environment or mental guides to help them find their way around complex buildings. Color can help to attract or direct attention to different aspects and features of complex materials such as maps and diagrams, and can thus serve as an aid to learning and performance. The different arousal properties of colors can also be useful. Warm colors, because they are arousing, facilitate activity and may help certain tasks. The wrong colors under the wrong circumstances can, however, be a hindrance to learning. It has been found that some people prefer cooler colors when working on complicated mental tasks, while warmer colors are often preferred when doing boring, repetitive things.

Color has been found to affect behavior under certain circumstances. Work with the mentally ill has indicated that different coloured lighting can produce different reactions and patterns of behavior among patients. Specific examples of this were that magenta had a quieting effect in one study, while its replacement with white light after one month caused patients to get much more excited. Blue had a prolonged quieting, soothing effect which was noticed by staff and patients alike. Yellow used with depressed patients had a slight stimulating effect, and red produced even more stimulation.

The color of ink has been found to affect handwriting. Handwriting with green ink is nearer to normal than when done with red ink.

The performance of factory workers has been found to vary with lighting color. One study which examined men working at factory machines, measured output under different colored lights. White was best, while colored lighting produced signs of nervous excitement. There was no evidence of a stimulating effect of red or a soothing effect of blue.

This is the bottom line. Color affects behavior only tangentially, spasmodically, and in the short term by affective and cognitive mechanisms. That is, moods and memories are most obviously affected by color. There are clear and consistent findings on color associations and preferences.

Thus color can indeed be used effectively to change stimulation levels and memory, improve signage, communicate urgency and safety, and, of course, improve the aesthetic beauty of the environment.

But there is no evidence to suggest that color works in more subtle ways on the human psyche; your perceived gravitas will not be affected by the particular hues in your tie.

The psychology of promotional products

Promotional products: Kitsch "n" tat or cost-effective marketing? Glance at your desk, your briefcase, or your closet and there is a good chance you are a proud possessor of a promotional product.

Mugs and mousepads, pens and polo shirts, caps, cups and clocks, brollys, briefcases – they are all promotional goods. It's big business and it's growing.

In 2000 American companies spent $17.8 billion on give-away toys and trinkets. For the UK, it is possibly around a fifth of that: but that is still serious money.

There are three fundamental questions to be asked by any potential client in this area. What's the main purpose/theory behind the enterprise? Is there any evidence that it "works"? And third – if it does – what is the process that explains its success?

In essence a promotional product is a small, decorative but useful item stamped with a company's name, logo, message, and colors. They are all "giveaways". And the aim? To have the recipient remember the name; to feel warm toward the brand; and in due course, in the fullness of time, over the years, buy more of the product.

The idea is that these products are used frequently. Naturally the product promoters do some impressive sums. You give away coffee mugs. They cost you $3 each. They are seen five times a day. The life span of the mug is a year. Using your promotional calculator you can work out the "cost per impression" (CPI): that is, for someone to read your brand name.

You can do this sum for each product and work out your CPIs. How many times per day will people look at your logo on a (good quality) watch with a three-year warranty? How often will they sport a good golf umbrella for all to see? If you give them playing cards, how many times over a bridge rubber will the players see your name? And, most cost effective of all, what about the (very, very, cheap) notepad with 50 impressions of your company?

Interestingly, if you play the CPI game there seems to be a nice linear relationship between cost of product and impression. The watch example works out at around .005 pence per impression, which in advertising terms is very, very good value for money.

A series of promotional product decisional steps is recommended as the route to finding the ideal promotional product. First, the purchaser is asked to define a specific objective. This involves thinking through the central theme and message. What promotional products bear a natural relationship to the branded product/service and the theme? A pharmaceutical company should choose something different from a bank or a management consultancy. Or should it? What is the message from a logo-ed watch compared with an umbrella?

Then there is the issue of the distribution channel. How do you get the promotional product to the right people, cheaply and efficiently? How can you ensure they will use it as intended?

The second hard question is: what is the quality of the evidence that it all works? Disinterested researchers have attempted to answer this central question. There are both attitudinal and behavioral data which hopefully are linked. One well-designed and very well celebrated study found positive results. A book company responded to teachers who had bought books in one of three ways: a third were sent a thank you letter, a third a letter with a cheap highlighter pen, and a third a letter and a calculator. Sales staff then called on the customers, who were later asked to rate them. Those who received the calculator rated the sales staff a third higher than those sent just the letter.

Another American study showed that customers of "Avon-type" ladies who were left promotional gifts were more likely to provide good referrals of friends, who later actually bought the product, than those who were left giftless.

But attitudes may or may not feed the bottom line. Other studies have produced positive behavioral results. One dry cleaning business compared those who received promotional goods with those who received coupons for their custom. The promotional product groups patronized the store 50% more than the coupon groups and spent 27% more money – which is what really counts.

There are also data to show that employees of companies that give promotional products as rewards worked hard – hopefully more productively – to win these awards. Indeed, the employee rewards and incentives business is one of the fastest growing "divisions" of the promotional product industry. Skeptics, methodologists, and social scientists may be less enthusiastic about the evidence supporting the monetary efficacy of promotional goods, and the research evidence is certainly not watertight.

But if promotional products work, the question is why? How does a cheap trinket lead to greater loyalty?

Certainly they have a "top-of-mind", prompt, psychology of memory, frequency-of-seeing-the-brand-name power. But there are better explanations in the psychology of gift-giving and the powerful and persuasive *norms of reciprocity*. Gifts of all sorts, be they that most elusive of all phenomena, the free lunch, to expensive presents, get us entangled in that murky web of obligations.

The reciprocity rule is deeply entrenched in our culture. It is the oil of social relationships. I send you a birthday card or a Christmas present; I buy you a drink or a meal; I do you a favor or invite you home for a meal … and you feel the need to return the favor. Hence the "much obliged" or "I owe you" response. Those who break this fundamental social rule are labeled "free loaders", "scroungers", or "moochers". Regardless of the size, cost, or value of the "gift", we are socialized into the reciprocity norm. You give me something (a trinket), I give you something (my custom).

On another level, the product has to be "right" and show an understanding of the recipient's tastes and values if it is to work as a gift. It must be something the recipient will enjoy/use/value and not, at the other extreme, give offence and actually damage the client relationship.

There are other reasons why promotional products work. Many firms prohibit staff from accepting expensive gifts from suppliers for fear of bribery. Yet such customers are able happily to accept inexpensive products. Promotional products need to have all the properties of a gift, but with the monetary dimension removed.

What are the properties of the effective gift? Many are ingenious thereby attracting attention: they have novelty, play-value, uniqueness, and utility. They have rarity value, for you cannot buy them in shops. They may be very fashionable or high-tech. Often they are simply fun, appealing to the inner child: the pen shaped as an aeroplane, the corporate teddy, the stress balls. Some of these become collector items: the BA washbag (traded on eBay); the Viagra key ring!

Another immensely attractive feature is collectibility. Some promotional gifts come in (displayable) sets. Again, they can only be obtained from the client and once you have started collecting you get hooked. Of low intrinsic value, but small, pretty, and displayable, they are seriously attractive to many.

Never forget the "snob value" of certain branded gifts, despite the oxymoron implied. The Concorde tie-pin, the Rolex cuff links all say I am rich, successful, important.

But most of us can quote examples of serious errors: where the corporate giveaway went horribly wrong. The company simply failed to understand their customers and their needs. Alas such incidences are highly memorable, perhaps even more so than when they get it absolutely right.

Glance around your desk. Are your pens, pads and executive toys essentially promotional giveaways? Which are the most useful and why? Does it make you favorably disposed to the company that gave it to you? And what have you thrown away moments after being "gifted" by something that was worthless, pointless, junk?

A marketer's dream: low monetary value yet high marketing impact? Get it right and you could do very nicely. Get it wrong and the whole thing could backfire.

The public sector

Compare and contrast people who work in the public and private sectors. An old chestnut? An opportunity only for creating stereotypes, straw men and bogus distinctions? Or a useful HR exercise in deciding why individuals choose certain jobs, the effect those jobs have on them, and whether, indeed, they are in the right sector for them?

The private–public distinction is clearly political: right-wing people support increasing privatization and left-wing people nationalization or some equivalent. So depending on where you are coming from this distinction is clearly good–bad, black–white, competent–incompetent.

From those in favor of privatization the distinction is clear. People who choose the private sector are brighter, quicker, better organized. They believe in the work ethic and most of all are customer responsive because they know the customer pays their bill. They are (healthily) competitive, innovating, change oriented, and keen on lean-mean management ... because they have to be.

In contrast people in the public sector seem metaphorically fat and lazy. They are slow, bureaucratic, and more into their personal work–life balance than customer needs. They are also risk averse, rule driven ... and deeply inefficient.

Those from the opposite camp, the pro-nationalization, public sector see those who chose the private sector as selfish, egocentric, uncaring, and unsupportive. They suspect they are being cheated by those only interested in their personal welfare. They aspire to being FAT CATS, who believe those at the top are motivated by reward and those at the bottom punishment.

Public sector supporters see their own group as sharing and caring; cooperative and supportive; equalitarian and fair. People in the public sector believe in public service and are prepared for personal sacrifice: service above self and all that.

Thatcherism in the United Kingdom heralded a new era with a clear private over public bias. The pendulum has however swung back. But more than that the difference between the two is much less clear. The public sector has taken on many private sector practices – and (to a lesser extent) vice versa. Public sector organizations are now run by people with a history in the private sector. Employees from both sectors move back and forth depending on their needs, the state of the economy, and so on.

There may be some dinosaurs from the old era that seem to typify both camps but they are few and far between.

Some people are clearly happier in the one sector compared with the other. Is this a function of their abilities and personality or their beliefs and values? Clearly there is much variation within and between each sector but it is probably the case that there is no systematic difference between the people in terms of their abilities or personalities.

But there is most certainly in terms of their values. Indeed the differences may grow as one stays long in one sector. Researchers have distinguished between values to do with the *means* of achieving something (or instrumental values) as well as *ends* (or terminal values). Consider the following list of instrumental values:

Ambitious	(hard-working, aspiring)
Broad-minded	(open minded)
Capable	(competent, effective)
Cheerful	(lighthearted, joyful)
Clean	(neat, tidy)
Courageous	(standing up for your beliefs)
Forgiving	(willing to pardon others)
Helpful	(working for the welfare of others)
Honest	(sincere, truthful)
Imaginative	(daring, creative)
Independent	(self-reliant, self-sufficient)
Intellectual	(intelligent, reflective)
Logical	(consistent, rational)
Loving	(affectionate, tender)
Obedient	(dutiful, respectful)
Polite	(courteous, well-mannered)
Responsible	(dependable, reliable)
Self-controlled	(restrained, self-disciplined)

Go down the list. Where are the public/private values most apparent? Helpful? Independent? Responsible? Self-controlled? Possibly, but the exercise is not that apparently simple. Now try the terminal values given below:

A comfortable life (a prosperous life)
An exciting life (a stimulating, active life)
A sense of accomplishment (lasting contribution)

A world at peace (free of war)
A world of beauty (beauty of nature and the arts)
Equality (brotherhood, equal opportunity for all)
Family security (taking care of loved ones)
Freedom (independence, free choice)
Happiness (contentedness)
Inner harmony (freedom from inner conflict)
Mature love (sexual and spiritual intimacy)
National security (protection from attack)
Pleasure (an enjoyable, leisurely life)
Salvation (saved, eternal life)
Self-respect (self-esteem)
Social recognition (respect, admiration)
True friendship (close companionship)
Wisdom (a mature understanding of life)

This seems much easier. Equality? Freedom? Social recognition? But still not easy. Confronted with these sorts of lists what is apparent is that people in the two worlds may not be that different. Certainly the distinction between them is far more blurred than it has ever been.

Redundancy and layoffs

The British Chancellor (Finance Minister) announced in 2004 that 100,000 civil service jobs were to be cut. So much for job security in the public sector. For those who like neither big government nor bureaucratic processes this may even be welcome news. A good example of *schadenfreude*.

In the UK, the 1980s were times of mass layoffs mainly from the manufacturing sector. Knowing someone whose job had been made redundant was not that unusual and there was much talk of what to expect and how to cope. We may have forgotten some of these lessons however.

Being made redundant, particularly in the middle years and without expectation of such or preparation, can be traumatic. It is a major life event, and an experience of major loss. Jobs give one status and identity, money and security, purposefulness and time structure.

Redundancy is more like divorce than retirement. It is having to cope with major change. Of course, depending on age-and-stage, personality, skills, and values, people differ in how they react. Some rejoice at the liberation. Others experience what is in effect bereavement.

But those who have studied the phenomena suggest that most people go through a series of *stages* once they have been "fingered" for the chop.

For nearly everyone there is *shock and surprise*. Nearly all believe the "could not happen to me" line which is often very adaptive. Despite the fact that it seems pretty apparent to everyone around that certain jobs are obvious for the axeman's scythe, few of them see it that way.

The first phase does not last long and may be characterized by some odd behaviors. Some express relief and optimism about the future: it is the best thing that happened to them; now they can move out of traffic-clogged, overpriced London ... and so on. Some put a brave face on it. Many go silent.

Some do complete *denial* and may not even tell their family and friends about their plight. There are always stories that emerge of people dressing for work, catching the same train, and wandering around the city all day only to come home at the normal time. They are really experiencing trauma and react in one of the most powerful and primitive of ways.

The second phase is usually characterized by *anger and resentment*. This is the time of union agitation, strikes, and sometimes attempts to sabotage the organization. Therapists know this phase well when dealing with the dying and the grieving. So do divorce lawyers. It can be ugly. Otherwise calm, rational people lash out against all sorts of people, even those that are trying to help them.

Then comes *depression* and its many companions, pessimism, fatalism, self-blame, and resignation. This is the difficult time. Therapists say one has to *work through grief*, for that is what it is.

But unless people are helped they can easily get into a very negative, self-defeating, vicious cycle. Those made redundant see themselves and not their jobs as redundant. They question their skills and abilities and begin to wonder if they will ever work again. This in turn affects their job search. Low self-esteem leads to few or poor applications, which leads to few or no interviews or offers, which feeds the low self-esteem.

Many suffer the classic signs of depression: lethargy, psychosomatic illnesses, emotional moodiness. Rather than take help that is offered, dust down their résumé, read the appointments page, or even potter in the garden, they seem immobilized by fear, guilt, and self-doubt.

With luck, support, and guidance they can move on. Existentialists talk of a "search for new meaning"; others of reality testing, and some of *acceptance*. The redundant have to accept that they must, and have, moved on. They are no longer civil servants although some may seek employment back in that sector.

The past is another country: they do things differently there. Redundancy can bring opportunities but they need to be sought out.

Research and policy

For some, no doubt, the dreary world of research and the near obsessive activity of drawing up public policy are equally boring. The image of those engaged in these two different worlds is equally unappealing: the inadequate, otherworldly scientist and the pedestrian, inflexible bureaucrat.

There are other, more appealing, although equally quirky prototypes of both groups. Some scientists, often those who find their way onto our screens, may be amusing, avuncular figures whose passion for their science and odd mannerisms can make them loveable boffins. There is no real equivalent for lovable, policy-making civil servants.

Boffins encounter bureaucrats when governments decide we need legislation. A good example is the current near hysteria over binge drinking in Britain. Scenes of rowdy, drunk, out-of-control louts late at night destroying property and defying authority lead to loud calls for something to be done. Votes are at stake, so governments respond.

Experts are consulted – people who, through their research, study the phenomenon. They ask, and try to answer, practical but complex questions. Why are there differences in binge drinking between cultures, nations and time periods? Why do some young people (and adults) indulge in binge drinking and not others? What part do economic, social, and psychological factors play? What is the causal pathway that leads to binge or addictive drinking?

The academic research always shows how complex these problems are. Multiple factors interact to explain rises and falls in social phenomena. In the case of binge drinking among teenagers, researchers have identified at least two dozen factors clearly implicated in the issue. While there is, inevitably, some disagreement among scientists from different disciplines, what is quite clear is that there are three or four factors that have considerable impact and a large number that play a relatively minor role in binge drinking.

Parents are implicated for two powerful reasons. One is their parental style – are they authoritarian or authoritative; overprotective or neglectful; moralistic or amoral? Parents model alcohol avoidance, use, or abuse. They may introduce household rules and try to enforce them. They remain the most powerful predictor of whether, when, why, and how often their offspring partake in binge drinking.

The other role they play is in the area we are getting to understand much better: genetics. Parents pass on their genes, which may be implicated in impulsivity, aggression, and proclivity to addictions. They also may pass on the particular way in which they metabolize alcohol. Alcoholism, alcohol abuse, and alcohol abstinence run in families through socialization and genetics. Binge drinking, destructive louts rarely come from stable, caring families who enforce social rules.

The second factor is peer group pressure. All parents worry about their children getting into the wrong group with delinquent norms and values. Adolescents are very prone to peer acceptance and rejection. They do what their peers do. They experiment with alcohol. They may be excited by its initial effects. It's marvelously disinhibiting. And "protected" by the group, alcohol gives the courage to defy adults.

The third factor is the young person's personality and ability. Some are extraverted, impulsive, sensation seekers. Others are sensitive and withdrawn. We have known for 50 years that there are distinctive personality profiles of young delinquents. They are aggressive and short-tempered, massively impulsive, often moody, and deeply egocentric. Disagreeable, not at all conscientious, tough-minded, and not-too-bright young men get involved in a range of illegal activities.

It has been shown, most interestingly, that group pressure leads one to start smoking, but personal factors determine whether one keeps at it. The same is probably true of binge drinking and criminal activities.

The fourth factor is culture. There are three drinking cultures in Europe effectively determined by where the Romans got to. There are the "wet" cultures of the Mediterranean, where wine is seen more as a food. It appears at most meals; children drink wine and water from an early age and, while consumption is high, drunkenness is rare. Then there are the grain, not grape, cultures of Northern Europe: "dry" cultures, where alcohol is about feasting and manliness. It goes with rape and pillage. Here there has always been binge drinking. And, in between, the "blended" cultures of mittel-Europa like the British, with elements of grape and grain; sensible and non-sensible; continuous vs sporadic drinking.

Parents, peers, personality, and culture are by far the most powerful predictors of when, how, and why young people are involved in binge drinking. After that comes the cost and availability of alcohol, and after that, advertising.

Enter the policy maker, energized by the politicians. You can't nationalize the family, although some governments are still trying. The policy maker has few options. Prohibition was a massive disaster. So the choices for control of drinking are taxation, licensing, advertising, and education. Increasing taxes has undesirable side-effects – smuggling, home distilling, the growth of booze-cruises. Licensing, restriction, and rules can work well, but need enforcement. Banning advertising is almost totally ineffectual, but gets a lot of votes. And time in the syllabus to educate the young about alcohol gets fewer votes.

It's a dilemma for the policy maker, which is why serious government documents have a worthy section on research followed by policy recommendations, with a yawning gap between them. After the prohibition debacle, the Swedes went the furthest to try to legislate against binge drinking through the usual means of high taxation on the alcohol content of drinks, state monopolistic control of outlets, almost total banning of advertising, and some education.

The result? The Swedish government appears to be recanting. Taxes have dropped and with them the relative cost of alcohol. But Swedes drink in the same way.

It's understandable why desperate governments lean on the policy makers to try to restrict the alcohol trade. "Something must be done."

Six of the best

There is no shortage of advice on what qualities to look for when selecting or promoting (but interestingly not when sacking) individuals. Books, newspapers, and magazine writers dispense recommendations and wisdom. So do consultants, but people seem more and more weary and wary of those spoiled brats of the business world.

Selection criteria are a bit like recipes: endlessly recycled, unscientific, prone to fashion. The world of evidence-free, old-hand, years-of-experience, business people means that untrained individuals hold the most bizarre ideas about the predictive validity of certain human characteristics.

Charm even the most experienced (even trained) selector and assessor and you can tease out the most odd of theories, all held with complete confidence. "Shiny shoes show personal discipline"; "Redheads tend to be hot-tempered"; "Football players really understand teamwork at work"; "Gap-year experience is the best index of maturity". Good old-fashioned gender, race, religious, and other prejudices are just below the surface but are beliefs that cannot speak their name.

Surprisingly, there is rather a lot of good empirical evidence on which particular individual characteristics are the best predictors of *long-term* success in *all* jobs. And they can serve as simple selection questions. Six of the best will suffice.

1. *Are they bright enough?* Call it ability, capacity, potential, or whatever, we know that intelligence is the single best predictor of success at work. The nature of the job dictates the level of intelligence required. Harrier pilots need to be much brighter than hairdressers; actuaries brighter than actors; physicists brighter than photographers.

    Intelligence predicts the ability to learn new things. It predicts how quickly and accurately people solve new problems. It predicts reactions to change. And it is associated with self-confidence.

2. *Are they resilient and stable enough?* Call it nonneurotic, stress-resistant or the nonworrying type. In an age of work-stress-blighted absenteeism, people believe that stress comes from the outside. Stress is supposedly caused by a bad boss, demanding customers, unhelpful colleagues, poor equipment, an unhappy work–life balance. But people react to stress differently: some adapt, others go absent; some

are rational, others emotional. Some are prone to anxiety, depression, hypochondriasis. Best pass them over – they are very expensive in the long term.

3. *Are they conscientious and hard-working enough?* Call it diligent, dutiful, the work ethic, or what-you-will, it is a very desirable trait. Some people go the extra mile without being asked. They stay late during a crisis; they forgo their lunch hour; even come in on weekends when required. Conscientiousness is about integrity and honesty. Too much of it can be manifest in workaholism, bigotry, and obsesssion-ality, but not enough of it can be really bad news. Those too low in conscientiousness are fickle, lackadaisical, and seem to have no drive. Harness the achievement-striving of the conscientious and you can really motor.

4. *Are they hungry enough?* This is about those dark, complex, even con-flicting forces we call motivation. People are motivated to achieve power, respect, or freedom through money, promotion, and other signs of success. Motivation is important but there are three caveats. *First*, is it healthy? The desire to vanquish others, to be respected at all costs, to come first in every race has a negative side. *Second*, are they realistic? Are they ever achievable? Short people cannot be tall however big their sports cars. *Third,* are they temporary and fickle, or long-term issues? This is mainly about how bright the light burns and for how long.

   Ambition is good. Need for achievement and success is very desir-able. They are both engine and rudder. Lacking them can be evidence of wasted talent. Fortune favors the ambitious.

5. *Are they educated or educatable enough?* This is about learning, edu-cation, knowledge, and attitudes to change. Like all the above, too much and too little may be equally undesirable. Lots of factors deter-mine a young person's quality and quantity of education. Parents' money, ability, geographic location – all influence how far a person has gone up the educational ladder. But it is equally true with constant change: we are all in the business of lifelong learning.

6. *Are they honest enough?* What people most want and value in their boss is integrity. They want to be told the truth, however unpalatable. Likewise employers want their staff to understand the difference between right and wrong, the letter and the spirit of the law, and accept-able and unacceptable behavior. Hence the growth in integrity testing.

Note the word "enough" in all the above criteria. It implies a cut-off point, like being tall enough to be a policeman or cabin crew assistant. Above that cut-off and it is less important; below and you may have a problem. Worse, you can compensate by being, for instance, super bright but rather unstable. Good candidates have to reach the prescribed level on all the six criteria.

Note *all* six critera. Beware the temptation to introduce a compensatory system where somehow scoring very high on one criteria "sort of" makes up for a low score on another. That way leads to doom and destruction. And also beware the bride in church fallacy as she whispers "I'll alter him" instead of "aisle, altar, hymn". If they have not got enough of the six characteristics, don't kid yourself that a few training courses and good management will make up for this and improve matters. That only compounds the problem.

Space exploration

It has become fashionable to explain much of human behavior, even at work, in terms of sociobiology. We are indeed *naked apes*, whose apparent sophistication and development are paper thin. So much of what we do is governed by cave men needs and concerns.

Few doubt that we are fiercely territorial animals. Neighbors literally kill each other because of very minor infringements of plants, trees, and hedges. And we still laugh at the beach-towels-around-the-pool behavior of our European friends, eager to mark their territorial possession.

Space at work is always a hotbed of contention. Office size is, or was, a pure index of power. The view from your window (if you are lucky enough to have one) may be important too. How close or far from certain facilities (car park, canteen, customers) also makes your space less or more desirable.

The size, shape, and location of work space for many people is a result of accident and history. Certain spaces, be they offices, cubicles, or just desks in a room, are usually considered more desirable than others. People have, over time, maneuvred themselves, either with or without official blessing, so that those with most seniority or service get the best space. Strange walls of files and desks can reemphasize the distinction between public and private space; between my and your bit; and between good and bad space.

Architects, designers, and ergonomists are often appalled by what people do in offices to rearrange their space. They do things that go completely against the original concepts, clear aesthetics, and even common sense, let alone health and safety requirements.

Work-space allocation and entitlement really come to the fore when people move buildings. Take an intact department, even a whole organization with all its psychological complexity, and try to relocate it. Struggles for power and superiority begin. Old animosities surface.

The best predictor of friendship at work is propinquity. You get to like those you see most often. That is why you marry the girl/boy next door. Enemies we put at arm's length. Or, at least, friends become acquaintances, become strangers as they drift away spatially as well as psychologically.

So a physical move nearly always leads to a psychological move. Indeed, some managers use a physical move to attempt to achieve corporate culture change. Most often it is to save money and the change can lead to many unforeseen consequences – mostly negative if the move is from closed to open plan. The two central questions for managers are workspace allocation and entitlement. They are closely related and very "hot" problems.

Entitlement can be considered essentially by four options. It can be, and usually is, select provision of space decided by all sorts of factors: rank, task, history. Your work space can be a reward for *long service* or *task complexity* or because you did well in the past. Sometimes the criteria for space entitlement are explicit, but frequently not. As anyone who moves house knows, it is profoundly disturbing and surfaces some issues that have "sunk to the bottom of the pool."

Old animosities can arise over space entitlement debates. People feel challenged on how, when, where, and indeed why they work as they do. Things become exposed – all very upsetting. And answers to reasonable and rational questions are wrapped in powerful emotional overtones.

Another entitlement method is *universal provision*. Whoever you are, whatever you do, however long you have labored in this particular vineyard, you will get the same space. And it will more than likely be open space. Soon one can feel particularly exposed and vulnerable and rendered equal despite patent nonequality in input and output.

This democratic option becomes ever more popular despite massive resistance, special pleading, even attempts at sabotage. But it can be and often is enforced with a sense of ideological zealotry.

There are two other options. One is that space allocation is done by *workteams*. The team gets the space and works out between the team members how it is used. This shifts the problem from the manager to the teamleader.

The last option is becoming most common but seems to fly in the face of what we know about our animal past, our basic instincts and needs. This is *nonterritorial* allocation. This is not even the world of hot desking. It is the world of each day finding a space and working there. And it presents the same dilemmas and tactics as the holiday sunbathers who all want to mark their territory around the pool at least a day in advance.

Whatever the management gurus might say and whatever the explicit values of the organization (manifest in the "vision thing"), space entitlement decisions are often made on criteria that are not strictly democratic, fair, logical, or even profit oriented.

Space can be allocated by grade/level/seniority, by task or function, or simply by giving everyone the same. It is easiest to make an argument for doing allocation by task. Given the nature of the task (that is, complexity), or the nature of the tools, people need different space. Complex cognitive tasks might not need much space (except between the ears), but they usually require that people have a quiet (that is, nonshared) space.

Other tasks require frequent team interaction and the space can be designed to facilitate easy work flow.

What you do, when you do it, and how you do it seem reasonable criteria for meting out the cubic meters. There will, of course, be odd mavericks who claim that they can't work except under particular spatial conditions. This is usually somewhere between special pleading, flimflam and downright attention seeking.

For the ergonomist or architect, the task is to understand the nature of the work and optimal conditions, and design around them. Unfortunately this may fly in the face of organizational politics, powerful lobbies, and of course our animal past. The alpha male will always grab more space whatever he does for a living. There is always more to meting out the meters than meets the eye!

Succession management

What would happen if the company grown-ups (CEO and the board) were all lethally poisoned at one of their many "awayday" jaunts at a nice hotel? Would the share price rise or fall? Would there be rejoicing in the canteen and on the shop floor? Would anyone notice?

Most organizations say they think about succession management. Many apparently have a plan that takes many hours of HR time and effort. It can involve trying to understand current and future roles, the skills, attributes, and attitudes required, and who in the organization possesses them. Some organizations have elaborate competency maps showing who, where has got what level of what.

The rationale for the whole business of succession management is to avoid unnecessary turbulence. Succession planning is meant to facilitate a smooth takeover, where company operations, procedures, and processes continue as normal.

More than that, it is argued that good succession planning facilitates growth and change. The dynamic, forward-oriented young take over from the tired, past-oriented old. The balance of continuity and change, of progress and evolution, sustained growth, and quantum leaps in results is what the company seeks. Hence the plan.

But do these plans work? Are they worth the time and money? Can they backfire? Many succession plans have both contradictory messages and unexpectedly negative consequences.

Organizations speak with forked tongue about careers. The career is dead. Lifers are sad people. You are personally responsible for your future. Yet, for the lucky, they are in a succession plan. This plan also sends messages about the anointed and the chosen to the whole organization. This can have the very undesirable effect of making the chosen arrogant and complacent while those not in the plan become disillusioned and fatalistic.

One trick is to try to keep the plan secret but things always get out. Once people know there is a plan then, however vague and imprecise, the rumors occur which can be more damaging than revealing the actual plan.

Another problem with succession management is the same challenge experienced by strategic planners. Plans go out of date very quickly. The "whole" changes. It changes fast and in ways that are difficult to predict.

A subsidiary is sold; parts of manufacturing are outsourced; the demand for a particular product suddenly dries up or doubles. And, most importantly, people leave.

Good people – hopefully those in the plan – are mobile. Headhunters buzz around with attractive offers all the time … If a fifth of the top 60 or 100 leave every year, you need people dedicated entirely to keeping the plan up to date. Brown who was to succeed Black left but White and Green do not quite "fit the spec". So the search is on to line up the ducks in the succession order.

Who put the success in succession management? It is not as if the idea is badly flawed. People need to be helped into a new role to ensure they are up to speed as soon as possible. There are lots of ways of doing this. One used to be "Acting" Head or "Acting" Captain for a time to give one practice.

But there is a much more important role and activity that most organizations totally neglect. It has no name but could be called "Failure Management". Every organization has its share of well-dug-in, alienated, "jobsworth" types, who never pull their weight. Often sour, jealous, and deeply disaffected, they never made it to any succession plan. Perhaps their attitude and ability determined that; or perhaps they changed once they realized they would never attain their ambitions.

In some organizations they are thick on the ground. No voluntary severance plan finds them volunteering. No motivational seminar has any effect whatsoever. No retraining is taken up with enthusiasm. And few threats of redundancy work. These failures are prone to all the features companies loathe: absenteeism, strikes, go-slows, restrictive practices.

The odd thing is that when asked to list these people, everyone agrees who they are (except themselves of course). There is, it seems, more agreement about failure than success. Perhaps it is easier to see. Perhaps failure is about the known past but success about the possible future.

So why not failure plans? Why no failure management policy? It is not easy. It takes courage. Managers have to be resolute. But for corporate survival it is important. Paradoxically more so than succession management. In the meantime, make sure that the organization's catastrophe policy is enforced, and never book more than five senior executives on the same flight.

Suing screeners and selectors

Compensation claims and "ambulance chasing" lawyers have made the business of selection a nightmare. In America, the bottom has fallen out of the intelligence-testing market as a result of actual or threatened lawsuits, because the tests apparently discriminate against blacks.

Recruiters and selectors, even trainees, have had to become aware of the impact both of legislation and of political correctness on many tests. Tests of abilities and attitudes, of personality and preferences, of vocational choices and values, all apparently have to pass various screens to ensure they do not discriminate against women (or men); or the handicapped; or the aged; or non-English speaking people, and so on.

The theory is that tests of many kinds may discriminate all right, not only between potentially good and bad employees but also on other grounds, which is unfair, unwise, and illegal. Despite pretty minimal evidence on the topic the anti-test movement has gained sway and now selectors are wary.

Without tests (of any type), selectors and screeners revert to the famous trio: the application form, the interview, and the recommendations. However, both the former and the latter have been under the scrutiny of the politically correct police and lawyers, and thus yield far less information. There is now a variety of things you can't or shouldn't ask on forms: age, health history, and so on. Some would argue that application forms have thus become worthless in selection, because the most useful, potentially diagnostic, and differentiating information cannot be asked.

The same is true of personal and character references. Again because of legal suits, some businesses will only confirm that a former employee worked from date A to date B. Nothing is to be said about their work performance over this period, or indeed why they left.

So the interview has to be the source of everything. And this is where the problem is. Consider some more specialist jobs, those where the job involves risk: police who carry firearms; detectives in specialist fraud or pornography; those who screen others at airports; those who deal in secrets. How do you select reliable employees and screen out the bad apples?

So what next? An obvious answer: sue those who make poor selection decisions, who got it wrong, perhaps indeed through failing to use a test.

The Roman Catholic Church knows all about this. Cardinals, bishops and the like are all under the microscope for not selecting out and/or dealing with known pedophiles. The sin is that of selection: not spotting that an ordinand was potentially sexually compromised.

The question is how to get at the dark side of an applicant's personality. Psychiatrists would call them "personality disorders"; lay people "derailers". It means finding cold, callous, amoral individuals who have a history of lying, stealing, and cheating. There are other types however, equally likely to cause mayhem in a business. These include those with narcissistic, paranoid or schizoid disorders.

There are now valid tests and checklists that can help selectors find these individuals. The clever, good-looking psychopath is a potential wrecker of all businesses. They are hard to spot; brilliant at charm and weaving a completely believable story. Narcissists have wonderful self-confidence, again thought to be attractive. The paranoid seem attractive to organizations that themselves have more than a touch of that world view.

One consultant recently remarked to a client "Give me the money now; or give it to me later". What he meant was "Let me use valid and reliable and proven tests for selection at the beginning, or pay me in coaching, outplacement, or remedial training once the inevitable problems have been detected".

Testing is not a panacea. It simply helps, like all other data sets, to improve decision making. All selectors should be in the business of selecting in and selecting out. You choose the right; eliminate the wrong. And now you can be sued for both selecting and rejecting, whereas in the past rejections were rarely a source of litigation. Select someone who abuses children; select someone who fails to detect bombs; select someone who is an impostor; select someone who sabotages a plant; select someone who embezzles the company … and you could be sued by the victims of the misdemeanor. You missed a trick and placed people in danger.

It may be, however, that your problem with selection is not the legal issues: far worse than that, you may be systematically selecting people who through their indolence, sloth, and negativity simply grind the company down until it fails. And in this instance, the selector becomes the selected.

Damned if you do, and damned if you don't. The money now or the money later. Sued for errors of commission; sued for errors of omission. The moral of the story: decision making has its costs. And they are getting higher. Gut feelings, common sense, and "years of experience" are no substitute for good data. Psychopaths, pedophiles, and others are very difficult to detect. It is worth the investment and risk of spending money up front not just to cover your back but to make better choices.

Troubadours, minstrels, and gurus

Politicians, CEOs, and academics often have a better life after they have been "let go" than at the helm. The unreelected politician, the dismissed CEO, and the retired don, if wise, lucky, and with a sufficiently high profile, can easily enter the lecture circuit.

A nice lunch, a few shaken hands, a couple of kissed babies, and an amazing, if somewhat edited, version of one's story, lessons, and insights for 50–60 minutes can bag really serious money.

For five to ten years after their encounter with the real world, celebrity speakers wander the planet – as their agent dictates – singing for their supper. It's a good life: the money is easy, they still feel admired, wanted, and appreciated; and people seem to enjoy the tittle-tattle and flimflam that constitute the entertainment.

As the speakers age, so do their audiences. Some old celeb-speakers struggle on way past their sell-by date, until many members of the audience were not even born when they were last properly employed. Others try to reinvent themselves as business gurus or semipopular authors to sustain the limelight and the dough.

Nearly always having been in positions of power and influence, celebrity gurus tend to focus on leadership. It's a good topic – easy to talk about, of perennial interest, and important. Academic books on leadership may be research based, but they do often seem trivial. Our newly minted gurus can be entertaining and can sound profound.

Are these the new minstrels and troubadours of the twenty-first century? The minstrel and the troubadour were slightly different, but performed the same task. Minstrels and troubadours were singers, lyrical poets, and general court entertainers. They were peripatetic merrymakers for the rich of another time.

Twenty-first century troubadours may perform the same task, but have some rather special help. They may have agents, personal assistants, PowerPoint, and various props, but they know they are in the entertainment business. Those who forget this lesson may get rather serious and start believing in the profundity of their pretty ordinary stories.

It is when the touring troubadour starts to mistake a warm reception for total admiration that things can go wrong. The problem lies in their feedback. Like visiting royalty, they receive almost always nothing but fulsome praise for stories and ideas about how to lead others. Questions are reverential, not probing, and minor vignettes are regarded as sufficient proof that ideas work.

Troubadours are tempted to see themselves as philosophers, wise elder statesmen, or worse, gurus. Further, they can easily offload hundreds of their books at every "gig" as a condition of appearing.

The real problem for these newly minted gurus is that, if they put all their good stuff into the book, what is left for the talk? So stories have to be embellished and other "long forgotten" tales of derring-do marshalled to support the themes.

What the troubadour guru needs is a list of ideas. The seven whatchamacallits of highly productive heroes, five good reasons to become a CEO, and so on. Old ideas need three things: first, they need to be expressed in the language of today; second, they need warm Disneyesque stories to illustrate/prove the point; third, they must be effective/emotional and about people, values, and the like, not accountancy, balance sheets or cash flow.

So we get treated to "tough love" (or tough empathy), "unique intuition" or "customer delight". The parables or lyrical odes of the troubadour must reveal their true humanity. They are, or were, and others should be, honest, caring, inspiring people.

Some even go further by not only admitting their weaknesses, but actually exposing them. This is nearly all true bluff, false humility, pretending that strengths are weaknesses. Being weak, vulnerable, human – they often say leads – (paradoxically) not to contempt, but the opposite. Self-confessors are forgiven. Further admitted weaknesses focus criticism to specific issues.

In the old days troubadours sang of love and life, but they knew they were an entertainment. Their poetry might have had profundity in it (or jest, or mockery, or irony, or simple yearning), but the idea was not to act upon it. They delivered amusement not wisdom; distraction not advice.

The conference or after-dinner speaker should understand their role and be grateful for their fee. The booze and setting may lead their audience to be particularly appreciative of their performance. They must understand both that every entertainment is a tour de force, and that they are alas forced to tour. What they actually say may be profound … and maybe not.

The value of experience

Those who can do; those who can't teach; those who can't teach, teach teachers; and those who can't teach teachers become educational psychologists.

In the old days of the service ethic (as opposed to service economy) people were appointed and promoted on their loyalty – for hanging in there, for their lack of "defection". They were the good old days of LIFO (last in, first out) not FIFO (first in, first out). The word that summed up loyalty, long service, and dedication was "experience". When people in those old-fashioned, state-run businesses were asked why they deserved to be promoted, they said "experience". They had done their time, acquired sufficient knowledge and skills, and it was their turn/right for promotion. Experience was supposed to be the factor that led to good performance, rather than ability, effort or motivation. This is all very different from the rather frightening (but realistic) idea of the present tense: we are paid for what we can do, rather than once did.

Is the word "experience" shorthand for more skills, greater technical knowledge or expertise, more awareness and competence – in short, better performance? The answer, it seems, lies in three factors. First, the stability of, and change in, technology. Developments in technology in specific areas have made whole skill bases and art forms redundant. The Luddites knew the value of twenty years' experience as a Linotype operator, Gestetner repair man, shorthand typist or a host of other trades long since discarded as jobs are automated by computers. If the technology changes, if completely different rules and laws apply, it is like a change of language. A fluent command of Finnish or Aramaic is not too useful in rural Zululand.

In any area where there are fast and dramatic changes in the way work is done, it is likely that experience is of little use. It can in fact be a detriment: it takes time to "unlearn" things. Ways of thinking and doing become automatic. Consider how you drive a car – unthinkingly. It takes time to adapt to driving on the "wrong side" of the road. It takes even more time if the controls are different, or opposite to those originally learned on.

Where the world of work is stable, where complex technology does not change much, where knowledge accumulation is gradual and the move from apprentice to master is slow but solidly incremental, experience really is valuable. But what sort of work is like that, outside the domain of the master craftsman? The gurus tell us we live in a world of rapid change, which means the world of rapid redundancy and obsolescence. All that skill and knowledge – absolutely obsolete.

Some people in their 50s can use a slide rule; send messages in semaphore; tie complicated knots – all learned at school and in the Boy Scouts. And all obsolete skills.

Second, experience is positive when it is "rounded" and takes in the big picture. The Japanese know this. People are moved around the organization so that they get an altogether better picture of the business. They are "de-siloed" so as to prevent them becoming narrow. They might have to spend time in departments to which they are not really very suited. The less numerate in finance, the less imaginative in marketing, the less technical in engineering. The idea is to see what the department does, how, when, and why.

Narrow experience has been the downfall of many, especially when they are considered promotable to general management. Narrow experience often encourages stereotyping; us and them. It makes people deeply committed to the importance, the complexity, and the necessity of their own departments, and perhaps a tad dismissive of equally important other departments.

In this sense experience can, or should, cap growth. It's the problem of being an expert: it is knowing a lot about a little, and very little about rather a lot that is important. Thirty years in accounts condemns you to ten more: while five in HR, accounts, production, and sales is the right experience for a general manager.

The third caveat about experience is that "people experience" is probably better than "technical experience". If EQ can be learned (it's a big if), it is done through confronting the slings and arrows of outrageous workers. There are various types of rather unpleasant people experiences that are very useful: sacking incompetent staff; dealing with a morale drop during redundancy or layoffs; attempting to reduce endemic staff pilferage; reducing absenteeism.

Not all useful people experience is, or has to be, negative: encouraging and mentoring talented young people; representing the company in public activities; acting as deputy during an absence.

If it is true that people are a great asset, experience in dealing with them is crucial. That is why doing a simple service job (like being a waiter) is such a good thing for young people. It teaches them how to get a tip out of capricious, irascible, demanding customers. It teaches them the meaning of emotional labor and it teaches them about teamwork.

Experience comes in many forms. It can be narrow or wide; long or short; of people or technology; of change or stability; of hardship or privilege. The experience of knowing that one can overcome hardship and setback is important. The experience of significant change in how one works is important. The experience of dealing with difficult, deranged, and defeated people is important. The experience gained by spending 35 years gradually clawing up the hierarchy in the accounts department may be important if (and perhaps only if) it contains the above experiences as well.

More and more you are as good as your last (job) performance. It does not matter if you have had 4 months, 4 years or 40 years at the mast – it's now that counts. Extensive people (management and service) interaction across a range of departments (or organizations) with different cultures in areas that are not massively changed by technical advances, does help. That is the value of experience.

Victims of the future

Some politically correct people have banished the word "victim". We are not allowed to say victims of Aids or victims of alcoholism anymore although we may be able to whisper "sotto voce" that some are victims of a train crash.

This seems all the more odd when litigation-hungry people appear to be lining up in droves to get redress from various big organizations because they are victims of this and that. Thus, while victim status is sought by many, it is deeply shunned by others.

The problem concerns several issues: personal responsibility and control as well as recovery and change. The pro-victim lobby want to stress that they were in no way to blame for their plight. They were innocent targets of various wicked things like physical and verbal *abuse*, persistent *bullying*, unsafe *conditions*, faulty *equipment*.

"Victimphiles" are angry. They want compensation and redress for their pain and hurt. Usually money, it seems, relieves the pain. But public apologies might also be called for along with the scalps of selected managers, bigwigs, and other high-profile hate objects.

"Victimphobes" come often from those involved in therapy or development. Most know the dangers of fatalism and strive to help people change. Their message is that we can and must take charge of our lives; we make our beds and we lie in them; we can be our own worst enemy; happiness or its opposite is a matter of choice; suffering is your decision.

The job of many therapists, as they see it, is to help people understand the way in which their "unhelpful" and self-defeating thoughts and behaviors trap them into worlds of anxiety, depression, and illness. The great message of the therapy of our time, namely CBT (cognitive behavior therapy), is that changing our attributions and beliefs can alleviate our self-defeating behavior and all its consequences.

The two camps may not be totally at loggerheads. Some victimphobes may argue that people need to "work through" the grief and anger phase before attempting change. That is, that feeling and acting out victimhood is a necessary part in the recovery stage. It is something to go through, like adolescence. But not something to either dwell on or indeed seek out.

Both victimphiles and phobes are past-oriented. They are concerned with how events conspired to cause misfortune. The phobes however are equally concerned with the future. We can, they argue, be equally victims of the past and of the future.

The past may be another country where things are done differently, but the future is an unknown land. Or is it? Can we make our future? Possibly. But can we better prepare for it?

At a very fundamental level, people trust authority less than they ever did in the past. Even those most solid of institutions, the church, the police, and the judiciary have taken a knock. Bank managers and bishops, priests and professors, judges and generals are not trusted in the way they were before. You can't trust in the integrity of great organizations. Their promises for the future are more suspect.

At the two extremes there is a fearful future. A "post-government" world or a Big Brother world. Both require great self-reliance.

Self-reliance is an old Victorian word. It is a word of Samuel Smiles and latterly of Lady Thatcher. It denotes a world where people take personal responsibility for their current and future lives. Where they invest and save. How they make provisions for their old age; for their children's education; for the unexpected slings and arrows of misfortune.

It is unfortunate that self-reliance comes with so many political overtones. For many it smacks of selfishness, of competitiveness, and of egocentrism. But it does not have to. The self-reliant know when cooperation is essential. Most of us are interdependent – we depend on others and they on us. Together we can influence the future.

Victims of the future are victims of the present and of the past.

What to do when the axeman cometh

Downsizing, right sizing, capsizing are, alas, all the rage. Consultants advise it; shareholders welcome it; managers do it. They lay off staff. With all the heroic talk of being lean and mean, the occasional headcount cull is thought of as a highly desirable survival strategy.

Delayering levels of wasteful middle management and reengineering for flexibility are the rallying cries of the gurus. Managers opt for programs with inspiring catchphrases like "Operation Better Shape" or "Future Fit". But it all means the same thing. The organization chart is reworked; bits are "sold off"; functions are outsourced; and some things are just stopped.

And it is the nervous fifty-somethings who feel most vulnerable to the chop. Seen as expensive, set in their ways, slow and change-resistant, they often look ideal targets for the cull-master.

The great fear of many 50 (over 40 and under 60) year olds, particularly after loyal service to the company, is that they will never get another job. They may have a large mortgage, children about to go to university and be at the "peak of their careers" … and then to be given the old "heave-ho" is terrifying. The reactions can be intense and very varied: anger, anxiety, shame, and depression can follow quickly.

Like the English weather that can exhibit the four seasons in one day so the job-threatened employee may experience the full gamut of negative emotions in short periods. Some contemplate revenge, others suicide. Some take to petty pilfering, others attempt whistle-blowing, or even blackmail. Defiance and depression may follow in quick succession. And also resignations.

What the layoff-vulnerable need most is not a counseling course on how to cope but a prophylactic strategy to deal with this common problem. The list below offers tips for corporate survival. They apply not only to those periods of culling but for long-term employment.

Essential indispensability: This is attained by expert knowledge of how things work. Almost by definition this knowledge must be difficult to obtain. But most importantly the "grown-ups" must know you possess it. People have twigged to this idea with all their talk of knowledge management. The knowledge is more than know-how. It's not sufficient to be the only one able to get the generator going because people are more expensive than generators and old machinery can easily be replaced. Knowledge, skills, and expertise need updating and advertising. It's probably the best defense against the chop.

"Manage up" well: Inevitably, managers will have a key role in staff survival and may be asked to choose their remaining team. So get to know, understand and influence them. What are their foibles? What gives them stress? What are their strengths and weaknesses? Help them, support them, befriend them, and they will be allies. But no ingratiating; no fawning; no obsequious stuff. It must be adult–adult, not adult–child and it must be based on an attempt to fully understand the other.

Get the big picture: It is too easy and far too dangerous to become organo-centric – inward looking and interested only in one's own organization. Survival means forward planning – insight into the business world in general. It means understanding what skills are in short supply, now and in the future, and those for which there is a surfeit. The aim is to have one's skills set sharpened for the needs of today and tomorrow, not yesterday.

Supportive alliances: Just as the great powers in the last centuries formed mutual defence pacts, so individuals need to be able to count on others to support them. We all need emotional, financial, informational, and social support at work. But it's a two-way, reciprocal process: there is a skill and an art to building and maintaining alliances. It involves diplomacy and subtlety. It means commitments that are binding. But it strengthens an individual's position. The labor unions offered it, but they are now too thinly spread, too political, and too reactionary.

Optimistic confidentiality: Alienated, passed-over, and disenchanted, employees whinge, moan, and bitch about everything. The past, the present, the future; the management and the support staff; the canteen and the car park. They are no fun to be around, forever carping on about the smallest thing. Few people like or admire Job's comforters: those who create negativism. They are idle gossipers; snipers who soon create enemies. People who are optimistic, trustworthy, and confident are much better liked by all.

Real team participation: Because the British are a nation of individualists, teamwork does not come naturally. "Love many, trust a few, always paddle your own canoe." But at work we are interdependent: we cannot do things alone and need to be part of the team. In doing so one needs to be a good team player. That means pulling one's weight. Contributing to the morale of the group and thinking about tactics. Strong links in chains stay there.

Eschew hubris: Put your head over the parapet and you may get shot. Certainly be careful about being cocky with your colleagues. Arrogant, dismissive, self-satisfied people are deeply disliked by all. Your life is often as much in the hands of your colleagues as your boss, so humor and help them. This means, in effect, not boasting about talents or efforts and most certainly not trying to take credit for something that is not of your own making.

Keep fit: People who are frequently ill and absent often don't pull their weight and are not there enough to defend themselves. As one gets older, the grim reaper can take pot shots at one. But don't overplay injuries, handicaps, special pleading. There may be a lot of special legislation concerning sick leave but don't count on it ensuring your survival. It is, as we know, survival of the fittest.

Whistle-blowers

Whistle-blowers: courageous guardians of truth and freedom, or spiteful and vengeful squealers with their own agenda?

A whistle-blower is an informer; an exposer of secrets. Their aims and their motives are complex, and often contradictory. They can be motivated by ideology and idealism, revenge and spite, greed and jealousy.

Go to the web – that library of all knowledge and opinion – and you find many sites dedicated to whistle-blowing. Two things are striking. The first is that whistle-blowing is nearly always portrayed as an honorable activity. It is an act of the brave and morally always just. Second, there are many organizations of all sorts that try to direct potential whistle-blowers to follow a set path through some tediously bureaucratic maze to (in effect) prevent or reduce the whistle-blowing to the press. Again, whistle-blowers are treated as perfectly legitimate, sensible, and sensitive individuals.

Organizations are justly very worried about whistle-blowers. One person, whatever their motivation, can individually halve the share price. They can bring a great organization to its knees and destroy reputations that took decades to build.

The central question is the *motives* of the whistle-blowers. This is much more important than to whom the information is leaked. There are two extreme types that appear in the press and the academic papers: Heroes and Villains.

The first type (H) is your prototypic ethical idol. These people see wrongdoing and do something about it. Unbowed by personal loss (of job), even danger (from a retributive employer), these heroes do what has to be done.

If you follow the story (read "moral tale") they follow the HR rules to a "t". First they report things logically, rationally, and politely to their immediate supervisor in the expectations that the unethical or immoral behavior stops. It doesn't, of course, in the story, because the supervisor is lazy, corrupt or pusillanimous.

So our heroes go up the ladder with the same issue. And again to no avail. Thwarted by indolence, apathy, and disdain, our heroes feel they have no alternative but to go to the media. They are innocent, "Just David" against the "Wicked Goliath". They represent the honest, upright everyman against selfish, brutish capitalists.

Of course the story has a happy ending: it has to. Investigative journalists (now themselves heroes a la Deep Throat in Watergate) do their bit and the whole edifice comes tumbling down. Dirty tricks, illegal acts, bent bosses, ineffectual inspectors and the lot get their come-uppance. Our hero, on a white charger, rides into the sunset. The world is just: Amen.

The problem with the fairy tale (or is it a modern day parable?) is that it rather oversimplifies. Ethics, like the law, are complex. Thus pro-life and pro-abortionist both believe they are (exclusively) in the right. Ethics committees judge the acceptability of scientific research. But our friends the whistle-blowing heroes are the sole judges. Their ethical considerations are sound, correct, and simple. But it all turns out in the end, doesn't it? And therefore whistle-blowing is a morally justifiable, even required, act.

But there is another story. This time the roles are reversed. The whistle-blower is villain (V). And the stories or case histories of the V types are remarkably similar.

The story goes like this. Long-term employee WV (whistle-blowing villain) feels uncomfortably alienated at work. Passed over for promotion, publicly slighted, let down by unfulfilled promises WV types feel increasing anger about their plight.

WVs are often too old, too unskilled, too sour, and too surly to get another job. So rather than leave, they decide to take their revenge. There are various options open to them: going absent, stirring strike activity, sabotage ... or whistle-blowing.

In this saga, whistle-blowing is seen as an act of cowardice, not heroism. The whistle-blower may send anonymous messages to key media figures. Indeed, people in the media sometimes report the sheer number of calls they receive, many of which could be seen as attempts at whistle-blowing. The fact that such communications are bitter, anonymous, and lacking in facts means they are, happily, ignored.

Our friend WV is interested almost exclusively in revenge – even compensation. Some may obsessively document every aspect of illegal, immoral, unethical behavior they see. But they are the exceptions, not the rule. And when they eventually come to light, after doing immense damage to innocent people, they are hardly role models. They do not burn with integrity; they seem unable (or unwilling) to articulate their ethical code; and their personal history belies their claim to much status.

Do Villains outnumber Heroes? Probably. It is really a question of the number of alienated, vengeful employees versus the number of seriously corrupt organizations. No doubt everyone has felt seriously unhappy at work at one time or another. And, equally, it is probably true that all organizations break the rules, if they can, on things as varied as health and safety regulations to minute details of accountancy.

When people are alienated or seriously disgruntled at work they have various options. Some follow the "quit-but-stay", "work-to-rule", minimum effort approach. The more courageous leave. But some take revenge for what they often see as selfish, corrupt management with poor pay and conditions for themselves. Stealing and sabotage, theft and blackmail, and giving "secret" information to competitors are all options that some individuals consider. And whistle-blowing for vindictive reasons is another. It may even be an easy option compared to some of the above.

It is therefore equally unwise to laud or lament whistle-blowers. There are not only the two types of whistle-blowers as described. These are mythical stereotypes at either end of the spectrum. Most whistle-blowers have mixed and ambiguous motives. As do companies in trying to avoid their activities.

Perhaps it is time to blow the whistle on whistle-blowers?

Who is your tribe?

Anthropologists call them *tribes;* epidemiologists *cohorts;* and educationalists the *Class of ...* We are all Children of our Time: shaped by the prevailing values and conditions of our early formative years.

There are currently four tribes at work in Britain. The War Veterans, the Baby Boomers, Generation X and the Millennials. What is it like to manage or motivate them?

The War Veterans are mostly retired or retiring. They are in their 60s, 70s and 80s, although many choose to remain at work. They often see work as beneficial and a duty. Some organizations seek them out as workers. They seem more reliable and honest. Happier to follow instructions and less likely to complain. They know about "buckling down", "digging for victory" and "eating up their carrots". And they know about sacrifice.

Of course not all people who experienced the war, or those gray but safe postwar years, are stoical stalwarts of steadfastness. Safe ... if you are prepared to ignore Korea, Kenya, the Cold War. And many are far from entrepreneurial or imaginative. But they are not difficult to spot in and out of the workplace, by their attire, their demeanor and their attitude to work. Solid citizens who worked their whole lives with the same employer. Loyal, stoical and conscientious ... well, most of the time.

The Baby Boomers inherited peace and stability at first; then Vietnam and the threat of nuclear destruction. But they rocked the boat. Now in their late 40s and 50s, they were shaped by the heady years of the late 1960s. They modelled anti-establishmentarianism. They were angry young men ... and women. But there were also flowerpower peaceniks and some enlightenment seekers. They challenged authority everywhere and very nearly brought down governments. Followers of crackpot gurus (pun intentional), they tuned in, turned on, and dropped out.

While various American presidents talked of the new society, they set about creating it. They rejected all that parents stood for ... but were happy to be bankrolled by them. Their fortune was to be young at a time of great economic expansion. They had, and many seized, opportunities their parents never dreamed of ... to travel, to stay studying for years and years.

Many of this generation had a long moratorium between adolescence and adulthood, but eventually returned to work. They did not seek solidity and safety in big corporations or dull governments. They seemed more adventurous, happy to change careers.

But the boomers did value *education*. After all it was at the universities that they learned rebellion. They also valued *freedom*: to try things new, to have control over their lives. Once they got married and had children they seemed a little less radical, but at work they strove like everyone else. Many worked out that money bought freedom. Some were happy to buckle down to 20 years of hard grind so that they could retire at 40 (or 50). And indeed some did.

Most were and are good employees. A little quirky perhaps, still happy to challenge rules and regulations; still thinking about further education.

The next cohort were the children of the boomers. Generation X. They have never received a good press. Capricious, irascible, mendacious. Unreliable at work; surly and egocentric. Is that fair? Doubtful. But employers did and do complain about them. They don't seem to have the passion of the parents. They have lost both the service and the work ethic. Drifters and opportunists. Was it their unstable childhood in hippy campers? Was it their parents' lax attitude to discipline? Were their parents, deeply indulgent, responsible for producing selfish little (and now big) brats? Was it the grim 1970s or early 1980s with all that industrial strife? Perhaps.

People from Generation X are in their 30s. A surprising number live at home or are otherwise dependent on their parents. They are not very interested in changing the world, just surviving it. They don't do ideology. They certainly work to live and like all the talk of work–life balance.

At work, employers find they don't "go the extra mile". They expect rapid promotion without the effort. They are hot on their rights and rather slow on their responsibilities. They know the career is dead and tend not to have psychological contracts based on loyalty.

And what of the Millennials? Too early to judge? They live in a competitive, politically correct, multicultural, all-shall-have-prizes world. They get brilliant A grades but want to be newsreaders rather than news makers. Employers complain that, paradoxically, they have poor communications skills and a rather unformed work ethic. They ask in Kennedy's words what their country can do for them not what they are prepared to do for their country. But they're healthier and more health conscious. Post-materialist but not very religious.

Their turn will come to keep the wheels of industry turning … if they have not all been outsourced to India or China in the meantime. Optimists point to their lack or prejudice, their self-confidence and their sense of adventure. Pessimists notice their lack of financial independence and their lack of entrepreneurial drive.

Why do an attitude survey?

Climate indicators, morale audits, satisfaction surveys: they have always been popular with HR professionals and consultants. They purport to assess crucial employee attitudes and how employees are thinking and feeling. They are, it is asserted, a critical management tool: a dipstick, a feedback mechanism and, more importantly, a diagnostic of what should be done and when.

Strictly speaking, attitude surveys tell you about current conditions, rather than the causes of those conditions. They do not tell you what to do to maintain desirable affairs or how to change the status quo to achieve them.

Whether administered by the intraweb or old-fashioned paper and pencil questionnaires, the idea is to request and require staff to rate various statements or answer specific questions. Some of these are so-called psychometric questionnaires bought from test publishers. They claim to measure all sorts of important things, such as motivation, satisfaction, and commitment.

But they are of little real value unless these attitudes and beliefs relate specifically and systematically to relevant work-related behavior. So the fundamental question asked by social psychologists since the 1930s is, "Do attitudes predict behavior?" It's a favorite first-year exam question. The answer is surely important – before an organization commits itself to expensive survey work, generating smart reports in consultant-babble which may, in the end, be shelved for lack of relevance.

Inevitably the answer is a little complicated and has a few caveats. Let's begin with a clear definition of the question. Do attitudes (note the plural) predict behavior? In others words, do attitudes toward a brand of toothpaste, a political party, a proposed restructuring of the organization, predict how people will behave? Will they buy the toothpaste, vote for the politician (or give money to the party), or embrace the new work conditions? Note too that there are different, if related, behaviors that may be a consequence of the behaviors. And observe that the statement infers causality from attitudes to behavior and not vice versa.

For fifty years *four* things have been known that are centrally relevant to the question of whether work attitudes predict behavior. First, the issue of *abstractness–specificity*. Put simply (and obviously), in order to predict a particular work-related behavior (accidents, absenteeism, customer service), one needs to ask specific attitude questions. In general, the more specific the better. Next there is the *single–multiple* question/act issue.

Attitudes are better predictors of behaviors not behavior. If a range of similar behaviors is recorded and the results aggregated, attitudes are more likely to be good predictors. Attitudes to absenteeism, sickness, and the like, are better predictors of annual figures for an individual than one specific week or month.

Third, there is the issue of *situational–cultural* constraints. Certain factors inevitably shape behavior. Having an electronic swipe card may change absenteeism rates, irrespective of attitudes. Corporate culture may be so strong as to pre- and proscribe behavior of most members of that working culture, irrespective of their particular attitudes.

Lastly, work behavior usually is complex enough to relate to a whole range of behaviors. Thus how people behave toward customers may be influenced by attitudes to their bosses, a customer's wealth, age, race, and so on. Likewise, absenteeism may be related to attitudes toward one's boss, colleagues, shareholders, and even subordinates.

But over the past 20 years, researchers have found ways of understanding how, when, and why attitudes predict behavior. It's called the Theory of Planned Action and it has attracted a lot of research activity, mostly resulting in confirmation of the predictions. The basic idea is this. We know the best predictors of a behavior lie in three things: first and foremost, the *intention* to do or not do something; second, the *past behavior* with respect to this specific issue; and third, the amount of *control that is had over this issue*. Ask people what they did in the past; how easy/difficult it is to do something; but more importantly whether they intend to do something … and you have a seriously good chance of predicting the behavior.

So what predicts their intention to behave in a particular matter with respect to a particular issue? Again three things. First, *attitude*: are they positive or negative about the behavior? Second, *subjective norms* – meaning their perceived pressure from important others to perform or not perform the behavior (peer pressure). Third, their *confidence* or, if you prefer psychobabble, self-efficacy.

Those social scientists trying to both understand, but more importantly influence, healthy adaptive behavior have learned that attitudes do predict behavior, but that to be any good you need to measure other things: intention, past behavior, perceived control, peer pressure, and self-efficacy. Too complicated? Well, life's like that. If you are not prepared to go down this route don't be surprised or disappointed when your attitudes surveys have little relationship to what people do and how they behave at work.

Work–life balance is for wimps

Work–life balance (WLB) is a big issue. Woe (and that may mean litigation) betide the senior manager who does not pay at least lip service to this idea.

But when the boys are together they rarely talk about it. It seems to be an issue for HR and for senior (or not so senior) female managers.

It is a fact that disgraced or failed politicians resign to "spend more time with their family", but "fat cats" never justify their salary on having to give up family time.

It is however not difficult to see why WLB is of more concern to females than males. Most working women shoulder a far greater domestic burden than their male partners. Many are expected to be mother, homemaker, and domestic supervisor once they return from the office.

Males can sulk, read the paper, "come down" with a nice claret, or potter in the shed because they have earned it. But somehow a woman cannot.

Asked to complete personality, attitude, or behavioral tests, many working women ask: "Shall I complete this as I am at work, or as I am at home?" No man ever asked this question. Women, it seems, have to be two people: schizoid. And they are, as they say themselves, more "natural" at home. Home is where the heart is. And, of course, where your heart is there your treasure is also.

But it goes deeper than this. And it is not because men do not love their children or enjoy home life. For men, perhaps more than women, dedication to work can be deeply, even unconsciously satisfying because it (uniquely) develops and exercises abilities that constitute their identity and enhance their self-esteem.

For men, *you are what you do*. It is different for women, many of whom feel they are mothers first and marketing executives second. Identity is less bound up with business.

People at work are in the game of achieving two objectives: to get *ahead* of others and to get *along* with others. This immediately suggests conflict. Getting ahead is a striving for mastery. It is a sine qua non for success. He who dares, wins.

You get ahead by hard work, dedication, discipline, productivity. There is no other way save the three Cs: chance, corruption, and criminality. It's all about 99% perspiration and 1% inspiration. Successful executives are totally focused. They say so; the company says so; the job demands it. The mission statements and the "vision thing" promise total customer care and much else besides.

And totally means just that. The share price; the shareholder meeting; the senior managers' conference in LA or KL or NY … that's what's important. The aspirant, ambitious, achievement-oriented manager knows that you get ahead by total investment. People in the business are encouraged, if not required, to subordinate their needs to that of the organization. Hence the supreme values of duty, loyalty, and obedience become paramount. And all the senior people watch each other to see who is not doing their bit … at all times.

The getting ahead bit is important. You have to charm, schmooze, ingratiate – but you dare not get too close, too confiding, too caring, otherwise you may compromise your first desire to pull out in front in the race.

So wise executives develop a curious avoidance of intimacy. They tend to try to maintain their distance from others, so as not to be compromised or be made to feel weak. Sharing and caring is not something you do (even if you voice the sentiments) at the top. Hence the need for the executive coach who is a real and trustworthy confidant.

At work, senior (male) people have power, respect, and control. They often have PAs to run their lives, relieving them of all that humdrum day-to-day stuff like booking tickets, ordering furniture, even doing the shopping. This may happen for so long that the executive becomes quite unable to function without a PA. PA-dependent executives do not know the price of anything or have simple urban survival skills. And there is no PA at home. The nanny can't or won't do things. The executive becomes the PA at home. It's confusing, demeaning, tedious, and unrewarding.

At work one has unconditional, positional respect that comes with the job. There may be obvious as well as subtle indications of respect that one is accorded. One *is* someone at work. But not so at home.

Most of all there is control. Senior executives can shut off access from others. They can regulate their timetables. They can avoid what they wish and they can get others to do their bidding. They can break the rules. After all, they have idiosyncratic credit which is the result of their sacrifice.

But at home the opposite is true. Compare and contrast a Friday and a Saturday. Friday is structured, planned, purposeful. Saturday is chaos. There are domestic duties. One is chauffeur to the children. One might squeeze in an hour or two of personal leisure but chances are one is expected to pull one's weight in home improvements and maintenance.

"Thank God it's Monday" is not necessarily the cry of unreconstructed workaholics. Nor of the managers who do not love and value their family. It is reassuring to go back to a timetabled environment with support staff and a modicum of respect. Yes, there is work stress but it has its compensations.

So, for many, life and work are not opposites to be held in balance. "Work is more fun than fun", as Noel Coward observed.

Beware the emphasis on work–life balance. You may find your job has been outsourced to India, where the concept is not understood.

Working from home

Work is not a place you go to: it is something you do. But you don't have to be a self-interested architect, designer or office furniture manufacturer to realize that where you work is really important to your health, happiness, and productivity.

Move offices, let alone buildings, and you soon see the effects on your daily contact patterns with others, which in turn can affect all aspects of your life. Perhaps those who know this best are those who don't go to the office.

There are many semisynonymous terms for people who don't "go to the office": homeworkers, teleworkers, mobile workers. They inhabit the virtual workplace. And they are growing in number.

Companies and gurus have trumpeted all the benefits of this new work style:

- Less commuting time (and traffic congestion/pollution)
- Greater autonomy and flexibility about when, where, how to work (with greater productivity, satisfaction, and much less absenteeism)
- Better work–life balance (for carers, the disabled)
- A better talent pool (no relocating, retain valuable workers)
- A distraction-free environment.

But many companies embraced the idea somewhat more cynically, for the obvious bottom-line benefits. Homeworking can dramatically cut office costs: space, heat, light. Telecottages can help rejuvenate rural economies and get hero points for the company. And, even better, mobile workers can work anywhere and everywhere … airports, hotel rooms, and so on. Mobile workers can go to customers rather than vice versa.

But, like all simple solutions to complex problems, the disadvantages were overlooked. The overenthusiastic endorsement by futurologists was premature. They clearly did not understand anything about the psychological benefits of work. Work is a source of stimulation, social contact, identity. It gives time structure and an opportunity to exploit natural talents. But laboring in the electronic cottage (read the spare bedroom) can be the very opposite of good work.

Below are 11 problems, not all easily solvable, associated with working at home.

1. Equipment, bills and breakdown: who pays for all the work equipment? That is *everything* – computer, desk, phone (even air conditioning). What about phone bills? Who is on hand to repair and service equipment when it goes wrong? How does the helpline work? Who pays for the downtime?

2. Health and safety rights and protection. In the UK, there are EU and TUC directives on how to deal with "outworkers". Has an ergonomist studied the proposed work area? What happens if a (sober) employee falls down the stairs, electrocutes themselves, or has an asthma attack at work? In short, what are the insurance implications?

3. How can one instil or maintain the corporate culture? Corporate culture is, in essence, a set of shared values and behaviors that have to be absorbed, learned, and practiced. Must every aspirant teleworker "do their time" in the office before being allowed home? Should teleworkers be required to do "top-up-time" in the office to ensure they still understand the same culture? Should only good office workers be selected for/ allowed to work at home? In this sense, is teleworking a reward for proving you have absorbed the culture?

4. How to control, measure, and monitor the homeworker? Nowadays, this can be done electronically, but many homeworkers deeply resent this obvious lack of trust. Imagine one's chair being monitored for heat or weight; the computer for key depressions or even (yes – it's cheap and possible) a discreet camera. So, if that's out, how can the supervisor be sure his/her report is being done and the homeworker is not mowing the lawn, doing house-repairs, baby care or simply shopping? The answer is twofold: training, but more importantly, results-orientation. Electronic monitoring is merely obsessed with presentism. Performance management is about results/output. Set clear, reasonable, challenging targets and allow the individual to decide how to achieve them.

5. Fewer learning opportunities through observation, coaching, mentoring, and training. How to prevent the homeworker becoming professionally "stuck"? This may involve setting up special and expensive training/educational opportunities just for homeworkers. Distance learning may be possible but it is more of the same. People prefer to learn from others.

6. Communication with head office. Both parties can feel hostile, jealous and antagonistic to the other. Head office rings the home office and

there is no reply, or vice versa. Where the hell are they? Propinquity is the best predictor of friendship at work. You get to know, like, even marry those you work with and contact on a daily basis. There need to be formal guidelines, agreed and contracted hours, attempts to establish a clear tele-working work culture.

7. Exclusion, poor promotion prospects, out-of-mindness. The office homeworker is an outport; a colony of the empire; a forgotten person when it comes to climbing the slippery pole of life. They are not promoted to managerial roles because they don't manage. They just keep doing the same old thing. And, with the end of service culture and the promotion of performance culture, they can get very resentful.

8. Family and friends not respecting work time/space. People might be constantly interrupted at work, but by colleagues rather than children, neighbors, friends, and so on. They might know you "work from home", but don't see why you can't have a quick cuppa and a chat, or fix the broken toy or whatever. Individuals have to be disciplined.

9. Subtle and effective communication. Electronic and face-to-face com-munication are not the same. The subtle tone of, and feelings associated with, the content of any work communication can substantially alter it. Electronic communication is cold, often blunt, and gives little insight into the ambiguities of management motivation.

10. The mobile worker can be dangerous, annoying, and egocentric. The mobile phone in the car; the (hardly) discreet conversation in the train com-partment; the laptop on the airport lounge table can be bad for business.

11. There's no Christmas office party for the homeworker. Some feel guilty about having a proper lunch or tea break. Many really miss going for drinks after work. So homeworkers join support groups; rent cheap office space; join the Rotary Club … anything for human contact, networking opportu-nities, and a bit of banter.

It's not just about reducing overheads. It's a different style of life and type of management. And it doesn't suit everyone.

Workplace romantic relationships

How should the corporation cope with corporate cupid? Is sex at work (attraction in organizations, office romances, intimacy at work, co-worker affairs) a matter for HR policy? Can, or indeed should, one try to legislate matters of the heart or hormones? Should romance or affairs be dealt with in an open, adult way or made taboo?

Over the last 30 years there have been various studies on the topic. Apart from the prurient, the PC police, and the puritans, the argument goes that workplace romances can and do have an impact on organizational dynamics, which in turn affects outcomes – productivity, morale, efficiency. Senior people can lose the plot, take their eye off the ball, compromise their integrity. New channels of unofficial communication can be opened up and closed down. The appointment of favored sexual partners can seriously affect how people perceive the transparency and justice of the selection or promotional system.

It's not easy to get evidence on the sheer number of workplace romances within big and small organizations. Studies in large organizations in American and Europe found that two-thirds to three-quarters of employees admit to having (closely) observed a workplace romance in their organization. Only about 10% of people admit to having had one but a third later agree that all romantic relationships are initiated in the office.

It is really no wonder they happen. The best predictor of attraction is propinquity. If you spend eight hours a day in the presence (or near presence) of others, it is no surprise that you get to like and feel attracted to them. Why should the office not be a good place to find a partner? People with similar levels of education, interests, and values are recruited to organizations so the process of assortative mating begins at corporate selection. Just as good if not better than the junior common room, prayer group or bridge circle to meet a future partner.

Workplace relationships can be grouped and categorized in various ways, but two dimensions seem most crucial. The first is whether the two people are at the same level on the corporate ladder or not: pretentiously called lateral or hierarchical relationships. The second is whether the relationship is open (recognized, explicit) or closed (unacknowledged, secret). Thus we have four groups: two junior accountants, or nurses, or journalists, begin to live together and (in time) announce their engagement (open, lateral); the head of marketing makes no bones about his affair with a new recruit from sales (open, hierarchical); two divorced board members are romantically linked but trying to keep it hush-hush (closed, lateral); and the engineering director is secretly bedding his married secretary (closed, hierarchical).

A romance is different from an affair. The latter implies that one or both parties are married/committed to others, infusing the whole problem with an added moral dimension. The charge of nepotism can arise where people (say, husband and wife) are appointed together and acknowledge their relationship. Another concern – almost unspeakable – is whether couples "do it" at work … and this is more than a grope in the stationery cupboard at the Christmas party!

Inevitably, employers who are themselves having a workplace relationship are more forgiving or even positive toward them. Various studies have shown that female employees are significantly less favorable to office romance and sexual intimacy than males. It is assumed that they have more to lose although of course the opposite case could be made.

There is some evidence that when in lateral relationships job performance goes up, but in hierarchical relationships it goes down. Further, it has been argued that work motivation improves because workplace romantics increase their enthusiasm for being at work. Equally it has been supposed that workplace relationships can increase employee motivation because the participants feel better about themselves and are willing to work longer shifts in order to extend their time together. They may even get more involved with their work, since their "partners" are part of the job. Also, the increase in positive effect experienced by people in a workplace relationship "spills over" to increase their general level of satisfaction.

The more popular lay belief is that workplace relationships have a detrimental or deleterious effect on the work of both parties. Energy is wasted in a closed relationship in the effort of keeping the whole thing a secret and too much time is spent on "lovey-dovey" talk and not enough on "batch-production targets" or "customer response forms".

However, there are probably three factors that determine whether the relationships help or hinder factors relevant to organizational outcomes. The first is pretty obvious: how good the relationship is. A good healthy relationship must boost general morale, energy, enthusiasm, and vice versa. Put pressure on a relationship and you stress individuals.

Second, there are the corporate cultural values regarding relationships.

These are different from corporate policy, HR recommendations, or professional guidelines. The more that relationships are countercultural to the organization, the more the problem, and vice versa.

Third, there is the resentment by the nonrelationship employees who feel, rightly or wrongly, that favoritism occurs. This therefore means that while the happy pairs might increase their productivity and morale, these factors decrease for the majority not in a relationship. If nepotism leads to positive discrimination, it can lead to a lot of people becoming alienated and disengaged. Some couples go to great lengths to show that their relationship does not compromise their decision making.

Workplace relationships happen, full stop. Draconian legislation probably simply leads to secrecy, rumors, gossip, and false accusations. Being open, grown-up, and sensible is best.

Conclusion

Is it more difficult managing today compared with say 50 years ago? Nearly everyone believes that business life has become more complex, more risky, more stressful. The past looks so safe, so secure, so simple.

However it is not difficult to paint the opposite picture, particularly if one concentrates on turbulent periods like the 1920s and 1930s rather than the 1950s. People worked longer hours under demonstrably worse working conditions. Most jobs were insecure and conditions could be both dangerous and demeaning.

But from a management perspective, the central question is, has work changed, or have people changed? And, if so, what are the implications for business?

1. Change at work

Futurology is an inexact science. It is easy to mock those who forecast the future. As little as 10 years ago people were saying that in 2005 we would experience the *paperless office* with people working a maximum of a 20-hour week. In fact paper consumption in the office has gone up as have hours worked.

The following were predictions made less than 10 years ago. Of course we will have to wait to test their veridicality:

Work in 2020	
■ Shorter hours	■ One month per annum – no work
■ 25% work from home	■ Easier commuting
■ Business 24 hours a day	■ Online recruitment
■ Privatized automated roads	■ Entrepreneurial renaissance
■ Rail renaissance – 350 mph trains	■ Growth of friction-free capitalism
■ Space shuttle to Sydney in two hours	■ Personal digital assistants
■ Precautionary saving for nonworking hours	■ Massive increase in PC power
■ Virtual companies – 10% of FTSE 100	■ Community work one day per week
■ Contingent and core workers	■ Global personal networks

Gurus, pundits, and futurologists alike compare and contrast methods. They like to differentiate between an old, bad, disappearing world and a new exciting, hopefully better world.

Below are some speculations about the world of yesterday and that of tomorrow (or today). Many of these simplistic catch phrases can and should be challenged. Further it seems difficult for pundits ever to resist the implicit old = bad/new = good assumptions. Things change in different countries in different sectors for different reasons. Globalization, mechanization, and legislation have changed some jobs dramatically while others remain almost untouched by the 21st century.

Old World	New World
■ Wired	■ Wireless
■ Office hours	■ 24/7 – open all hours
■ Corporate headquarters	■ Satellite companies
■ Local/global markets	■ Web-based marketing
■ e-excitement	■ e-fatigue
■ Surplus of youth	■ Surplus of wrinklies
■ Departments and divisions	■ Flexible team
■ Paid for attendance	■ Paid for output
■ Attentive to boss	■ Attentive to customers
■ Boss is supervisor	■ Boss is coach
■ Boss is scorekeeper	■ Boss is leader
■ Command, control, and mistrust	■ Networks, self-managed teams
■ Labour, land, and capital	■ Knowledge, information, and response time
■ Fixed, hierarchical, stable	■ Nomadic, equal, flexible
■ Loyalty, compliance	■ Self-evaluation and responsibilities
■ Work/life separate	■ Work/life blur
■ Norms, customs, and laws	■ Relationships

Always there is a tremendous emphasis on what has changed and therefore what needs to change. Supposedly there have been changes in the *workforce* in terms of cultural diversity, skill experience, and expectations, which probably differ significantly from one country to another.

Changes in *customer expectations* have *clearly occurred*, which normally means a rise in the quality and reliability of products, and the excellence of service demanded.

It seems likely there are consistent changes in the *size, structure, and international focus*, and the managers needed to run them. Economic, legal, social, and competitive forces mean that companies have to adapt, reinvent themselves, and reengineer simply to survive, let alone prosper.

Inevitably there are macro sociopolitical changes in *economic conditions* governed by new inventions (the electronic revolution), raw material (the exhaustion of certain assets), and political cooperation and competition.

This change has meant pressures and challenges facing both individuals and organizations. Individuals have to get used to no more jobs for life. They have to think of work as something you do, not somewhere you go. They need to think of themselves as being employable, not being employed. And they need to take more, if not total, responsibility for their own learning and development.

Organizations face greater global competition, faster reactions, and reduced product life cycles. They face a different workforce and flexible workers.

The following seven changes are commonly asserted:

1. The way we think about:
   - Ourselves at work
   - Our boss, colleagues
   - Our customers
   - Our shareholders
2. The expectations of customers
3. The speed, openness, and cheapness of communication
4. The cost, shelflife, size, and portability of technology
5. Our use of time
6. The working life in a time of greater longevity
7. Globalization of workforce and markets.

Equally it has been noted that there are various fairly consistent business responses to these changes at work. They include:

- A continual reorganization of various divisions. Some believe this can mean reorganization for its own sake. There is more subcontracting noncore services and operations. Businesses have learned they need to develop good relationships with key constituencies.
- Streamlining and rationalizing processes is an ongoing issue. People are being replaced by machines that are cheaper and more reliable. Subscribing to continuous improvement of processes is seen as a necessity. The Japanese concept of *kaisen* has really caught on.

Creating flatter structures is very popular. Creating more teamwork has been an issue for ages. Developing core competencies and jettisoning peripheral activities are thought of as fundamental.

■ Recognizing workforce diversity is seen as essential. Creating a flexible workforce is all the rage. Empowering people at work has been a popular slogan for ages although it is not always fully understood. Promoting the concept of the manager as a facilitator and coordinator. There has been a great deal of debate about the role of, indeed title for, managers.

■ Recognizing a need for employees to continually update their knowledge and skills. This can mean companies abrogate or even deny their responsibility for training their people.

■ And so we see companies have fewer core employees and more part-time, contingent, teleworkers. Indeed there have been all sorts of attempts to reduce company costs while simultaneously increasing employee productivity and satisfaction. Hence enthusiasm for teleworkers. Often the disadvantages to both employer and employee are underreported.

■ Another enthusiasm is to employ older (often quite old) workers. But is this a wise move? Are older workers less effective than younger ones? Across jobs in general there is no evidence of age differences in general effectiveness. Older workers are thought of as more careful, reliable, loyal, knowledgeable, and socially skilled but less willing to change. Further, absenteeism, accidents, and turnover are higher with younger staff.

All this talk of change is at once anxiety provoking and boring. It is anxiety provoking because change is hard, even unnatural. It is difficult to change one's own attitudes and behaviors and even more so those who do not want to be changed. The older one is the more difficult it is to change. And all this change talk is boring. People go on about it remorselessly. It has been suggested that all management is indeed the management of change. But for all the above it is a necessity, not an option. Adaptation to a new environment is a requirement of keeping in business.

People may be different in their attitudes, beliefs, and values but not in their fundamental psychological processes. To some in the West it seems that young people are different. They are better educated (overall) and more knowledgeable about business. They seem more confident, socially skilled, and know they need to be self-motivated. They probably have useful, indeed necessary, experience of teamwork. But they still want their bosses to be honest, bright, and inspiring. They still need to be clear about their goals and they need support in achieving them. And they need constant feedback on how they are doing.

The Emotional Intelligence revolution has meant that employers seem to emphasize more the soft skills of business. These include interpersonal skills that seem to be associated with communicating, influencing, leading, and teamwork. They also emphasize intrapersonal skills associated with motivation, self-management and problem solving.

It is possible to describe different work–life trajectories or types. Consider the following five:

Drifters: Directionless, unambitious, fickle, restless, reckless
Lifers: Loyal, risk averse, seniority-based/service ideology
Hoppers: Snakes and ladders experience with no vision
Planners: Carefully planned and managed (headhunters, résumé)
Hobbyists: Sobos (shoved out, but better off), willing to trade off ambition for lifestyle.

Attitudes, beliefs, and values do shape (predict) behavior. They determine in part the sorts of jobs people seek and shun; those that they revel and rebel in; and those where they may be optimally productive or unproductive. They shape expectation which influences behavior.

Does this mean people are fundamentally different or have to be managed differently. The answer is in part yes. Managers have to be aware of and then shape expectations. A new workforce in a new workplace needs guidance as to what is expected of them and why. If workgroups are better educated, more diverse, and less stable, managers will themselves need to take these factors into consideration.

The job of management has probably gotten more difficult. As work becomes more complex, organizations more flexible, and people both more able and more demanding, managers have to be able to respond. But it does not mean that the most fundamental tasks of managers are any different than they were 100 or 1000 years ago. People need clear, stretching, clear, explicit targets and goals. They need moral, technical, social help and support in achieving those goals. And they need honest, accurate, regular, feedback on how they are doing.

2. Spotting and managing talent

As well as managing change, it is the fundamental job of managers to recruit and retain talented people – people who are adaptable, self-motivated, productive, happy, and loyal. It has been said there is a "war for talent", meaning that because of the supply–demand issue there are far more people chasing talent than actually exists. There are various descriptions of talented individuals: high potential, high flyers, wunderkinds.

A great deal of business is about risk assessment. Whether it is the development of a new process or product, or the introduction of a new system or structure, all businesses have to attempt to analyze market trends, anticipate changes and innovations, and respond appropriately. Although not always thought of in these terms, the business of development, recruitment, selection, and succession planning is also about risk assessment. This is equally done when promotion or succession planning decisions have to be made. While there is inevitably risk in choosing the preferred selection/assessment method and an issue as to the appropriate level of resources (people and money) put into the decision process, there is clearly risk involved in choosing any organization's "most valuable asset" ... people.

Assessing the potential for an individual to succeed, even flourish, in a particular demanding and crucial job, and in a series of more senior jobs thereafter, is essentially an actuarial type decision. The assessment of managerial potential has three fundamental issues to consider:

- First, what is talent? What personal characteristics need to be assessed and why? Just as actuaries have a clear idea of risk factors for insurance (what they are, their respective weights, how they interact, and how common they are), so people assessors need first to have some idea of the individual characteristics that predict success in a particular job or series of jobs.
- Second, it is important to know how to gather the data. There is a whole range of possible methods one may use in gathering these data including self-report (questionnaire, interview, biodata), observation data (references, assessment center data, 360° feedback), and test data (ability, intelligence tests).
- Third, how can one help a person fulfil his or her potential? After potential has been identified, the question remains how to realize as opposed to waste or frustrate that potential.

Few disagree about the usefulness of spotting those with high potential. It helps identify those ready for promotion, and focuses on optimal developmental job moves. It can allow high-level succession planning and targets training efforts for senior positions.

Over time organizations tend to develop selection and recruitment strategies based on particular ideas. Consider the following unrelated but often widely held views: "You can rely on certain others to do much of the screening for you". Some companies only recruit from particular universities (Oxbridge, Ivy League) in the belief that the dons have done a good job both in the selection of the brightest and also in training them well. This naturally puts the onus on others to choose the selection criteria and apply them, but presumably if an organization has been pleased with "products" from these institutions they will continue to use this, very cost-effective, method.

The process for identifying "high potential" among applicants, or those already within an organization usually involves the identification of job skills and future needs of the organization through job analysis and person specification. The fundamental questions posed by the process include:

- What will future executive jobs be like? What staff requirements do they have? What knowledge base will be a basic requirement? In short, can we specify what skills, abilities, knowledge sets will be needed to perform all the major tasks in any job?
- What sorts of people will be required to fill these jobs? What will be their demography (sex, age); typical educational background; skill-set and personality traits. Will they be able to adapt to changing circumstances? Can they cope with stress and welcome change?
- What are the best methods to identify high potential? How can one best evaluate the usefulness of these different methods? What particular biases and limitations do different methods have? Are biodata more cost effective and accurate than having an assessment center? Are interviews really of no validity whatsoever?

The assessment of potential means not only attempting to optimally match people for jobs but deciding how both may change in the future. Many organizations have the concept of a "fast stream" of young, recently hired individuals who have been labeled as those with potential to "go far", meaning get rapid, but deserved, promotion. They are usually sought after for their intelligence, temperaments, but most of all their motivation and flexibility. Given that the future is unclear but notably different from the present, the successful employee will be able to anticipate, adapt to, and thrive in a different working situation from the one he/she was specifically chosen for.

Speculating on the nature of future jobs is an important yet problematic issue in the selection of high flyers and those with potential. This may be done by an examination of current management jobs and seeing trends and changes in the past which are projected into the future. Another method may be to look at generic lists of identified managerial competencies or capabilities. It may also be advisable to seek out explicit opinion from technical experts and futurologists.

The problem of using the past and the present to evaluate and predict the future is nicely summarized by Spreitzer et al. (1997, p. 6).

> Yet executive identification and selection systems based on end-state competencies alone are likely to be double edged. When they are carefully developed and connected to the business strategy, the resulting set of defined and internally accepted competencies can be invaluable. However, because the origins of competencies are based on past success rather than future challenges, their value for the early identification of executives may be limited. We risk choosing people who fit today's model of executive success rather than the unknown model of tomorrow. The competencies that get attention today may not be enough to ensure that a person will master requisite competencies for the future. Given that future demands may include some skills that are different from the skills values today, the ability to learn from experience may prove to be more important in the long run than a high rating in a currently valued competency. Thus, to the degree that executive leadership skills are learned from experience, any improvement in identifying people who can learn more from their experiences is likely to aid in the early identification of international executives.

In their study they identified 11 signs of success: early identification of talent. They were:

1. Seeks out the opportunity to learn: is educationally proactive; enjoys skill/knowledge acquisition.
2. Acts with integrity: is known to be honest; takes responsibility for actions.
3. Adapts to cultural differences: enjoys and is sensitive to cultural variation.

4. Genuinely committed to making a difference: willing to make personal sacrifices; wants impact on the business as a whole.
5. Seeks broad business knowledge: interested in the whole business; goes beyond area of professional expertise.
6. Brings out the best in people (particularly reports): has the talent to create effective team, working environment; understands individual differences, develops others naturally.
7. Is insightful even intuitive: sees things from new angles; quick to see trends; good at taking the perspective of the other. Seems to understand people's motives, desires, and aspirations.
8. Courageous and willing to take risks: is not afraid to go against the grain; will persevere in the face of opposition; can confront poor performers.
9. Seeks and uses feedback: actively pursues, responds to, and uses feedback to learn how to be better.
10. Learns from mistakes: changes direction when necessary; starts again after setbacks; not defensive to negative feedback.
11. Is open to criticism: handles criticism well. Understands differences between criticism of self vs ideas.

The assessment of individuals is based on a number of assumptions such as how much people change over time naturally, how easy it is for them to change, and how best to create an environment that ensures talented people with "the right stuff" achieve their potential.

An equally important and central question is what characteristics seem to predict success, and which methods are most sensitive, robust, and reasonable at doing so? The first question is do people change much over time: that is, can talent be trained into people?

This is a very central question for the adult assessment process because if people change a great deal in terms of their personality, preferences, and predilections, and one cannot control factors that cause these changes (or indeed understand the process of change itself), the business of future assessment is well nigh impossible. People can and do change over time mainly as a result of things: *traumatic experience* (death of loved ones; personal death scare; failure of marriage), *therapy* (aimed at radical cognitive behavioral change), or occasionally *personal motivation* (to give up alcohol or cigarettes, lose weight, help others).

Yet the evidence from the industry aimed at personal change (namely therapy) suggests that it is extremely difficult and relatively rare. That is, it is by no means easy, for any adult to change habits and outlooks once established. The reason for this is that many behavior patterns are closely linked to personality traits or skill ability sets that are themselves genetically linked. Indeed, the more we discover about behavior genetics, the more obvious it is that a great deal of variance can be explained by genetic factors that are themselves not much open to change.

Research findings suggest that for an adult of 25 years or older "what you see is what you get". That is, basic personality structure and functioning do not alter appreciably. Whereas jobs may change dramatically over time individuals do not. Latent talent therefore really needs to be found and allowed to flourish.

Next, if personality traits and abilities are fairly stable over time how easy is it to change them or a style of working directly related to them? However, the process of change and learning to adapt, at any age, is stressful. Learning new skills, or how to treat staff and customers differently, or how to face the ruthlessness of market forces naturally induces anxiety. It also causes problems for those who have to, or choose to, bring about change. "Adapt or die: change or decay" is not just a rallying cry for the senior manager. It is a reality. The question is how to bring about successful change to maximize effectiveness and minimize pain?

There is much industry dedicated to personal change. One form is dedicated to changing beliefs and behavior patterns to make people happier, more functional. This is counseling and psychotherapy. The other form is dedicated to instilling skills and knowledge; so that they can be more effective at work. This is training and education.

The conclusion is that personal change is possible but at some cost and investment of both the change agent (therapist, trainer) and the client of change. People can change – although the prognosis for some forms of psychological problems remains very poor. As a dieter or ex-smoker will tell you it takes willpower, support, and perseverance to change personal habits. Personal preferences, and pathology, are closely linked to work style, productivity, and outcome. Neurotics manifest lower morale, greater absenteeism, and often lower productivity. It is possible, but difficult and costly, to "cure" or dramatically alleviate neurotics. Training is often little different from therapy in its aims to change attitudes and behaviors. Yet the research on therapy and its effectiveness is better developed than that of training.

The question of identifying precursors of predictors of business success says nothing about how to ensure that the potential is realized.

Inevitably there may be reasons why it is important to give an individual particular tasks and challenges at specific points in their life so as to ensure that their potential for success is realized.

McCall (1998) posed the above question which is a variant of the "are managers born or made" question. He noted that "even if talents' origins are biological, bringing it to fruition requires years of hard work and conscious developments" (p. 118). He laments the fact that so many organizations strive so hard to develop a list of exclusive, and essential, competencies (a potpourri of traits, motives, values, behaviors, attitudes) that drive all the HR systems including selection. This approach has several shortcomings in that it can erroneously assume:

- The job will not change significantly in the short term
- The job has an identity separate from the incumbent and will not be shaped by him or her
- The requirements for effective performance in the job are exclusively described by the list of competencies
- The incumbent's actions, rather than the organizational-wide forces control the outcome
- The list of competencies can be found in one individual
- The competencies interact with each other to change the outcome.

In short talent (ability and motivation) is not enough to ensure competent, if not excellent, management. What is also required is appropriate learning experiences. McCall (1998) argues that "leadership ability can be learned, that creating a context that supports the development of talent can become a source of competitive advantage, and that the development of leaders is itself a leadership responsibility" (p. xii). He rejects the assumption that a shortlist of generic qualities can be drawn up to describe all effective leaders; that those qualities are stable over the course of a person's career; and that through survival of the fittest the best survive, requiring only a minor polish and refinement. He stresses that continual growth, transition, and transformation are as much associated with success as "natural ability". Dealing with adversity may be, according to McCall (1998), a better predictor of success than a seamless career of a "wunderkind".

In short he believes that "leaders are both born and made, but mostly made" (p. 51); that organizations need to strengthen and polish what already exists but also bring into being potential. He distinguished between two models:

- *The Darwinian Model* which attempts to differentiate less/more successful executive traits, search for the latter then give people tests/experiences to polish these skills. On-the-job challenges reveal actual talent
- *The Agricultural Model* which attempts to identify strategic challenges likely to occur and the search for people who can learn from the experiences, then help them to succeed.

To continue the agricultural analogy the following seems to follow:
How to *grow* a manager:

- First, select good stock or seed: make sure that you select the best people (ability, personality, EQ, IQ)
- Next, prepare the land or environment: notably where they are going to work (equipment, office, corporate culture)
- Enrich the land by weeding, watering, and fertilizing: make sure the physical and social environments are able to sustain goodwill (update all systems, deal with problem people)
- Rotate the crops: give people a chance to learn new things (encourage a variety of experiences)
- Occasionally let a field fall fallow: understand the importance of sabbaticals and times of refreshment (give genuine "time out" opportunities)
- Understand the preferred plant/animal environment in which they thrive (look for the best fit of person and environment)
- Look for hybrids to go one step further: seek especially hardy, talented individuals (seek out the unusual combination of talents).

In a sense he argues from survival of the fittest to the development of the fittest: from being a corporate Darwinist to a managerial developer. A number of experimental criteria are thought to be very good for development. These include job transitions (taking on unfamiliar responsibilities), implementing change strategies, taking on higher levels of responsibility, and being influential in nonauthority relationships. Developmental opportunities can arise from being given new assignments (project, task force), dealing with hardships/setbacks (business failure), other people (who are role models) and "other events". Clearly, people who take on continuous modest challenges with occasional change of function learn most. International assignments and training can all justify this process. Some organizations choose to have company schools and universities. Whether deliberate or serendipitous, organizations provide powerful experiences that provide an opportunity to learn.

The Darwinian and developmental approach are not opposites. McCall (1998) argues that one needs to select those with the talent to exploit their talents in order to assess, then realize potential. His preference is to focus on the range of developmental experiences talented people should have to develop their abilities rather than find those people who currently demonstrate these desired qualities. Others have argued that leadership is a journey of personal development and that derailment is the result primarily of talented people not learning from experience, or of course not having the experience.

Ultimately the question remains about how organizations provide the learning experience their potential leaders need. Most companies insist that managers are accountable for results and not development and hence ignore the development aspects of job assignments. Job rotation focuses on exposure rather than task. Managers need incentive, resources, and support to change.

What one needs is a model for developing talent. This is an explicit, systematic, and comprehensive attempt to take the developmental model seriously. This research suggests that it is the capacity to learn that is most important. Successful managers have to *draw attention to their talent* which results in better opportunities to develop it. They need to have a *sense of adventure* to take on challenges and to *create a context* for their own learning. And they also need to be able to learn from experience, respond to feedback, and bounce back after setbacks. In this sense one can pick people with potential by looking at certain characteristics that predict that the potential will be realized.

The search for and management of all staff is at the heart of the people business of management. It requires skill and knowledge at all stages of the career cycle: recruitment, selection, induction, production, and exiting. It is the heart of the business.

Every manager wants happy, healthy, and productive staff. They want them to be dedicated and loyal, committed and competent. Much can go wrong – from selecting the wrong people to inducing alienation in an otherwise productive team.

People are fickle and capricious. Further, they have one thing in common – they are all different and therefore have to be treated as such. So managers have to be strategists and psychologists. They need to keep their focus on the task, the individuals, the team … and themselves. They need to have vision; a long-term view. And finally they need to move from being a manager to being a leader: someone with energy, integrity, drive, and a vision.

References

McCall, M. (1998). *High Flyers: Developing the Next Generation of Leaders.* Boston, Mass: Harvard Business School Press.

Spreitzer, G., McCall, M., and Mahoney, J. (1997). Early identification of international executive potential. *Journal of Applied Psychology*, **82**: 6–29.